Dedicated to the lovely people of the village of Frettenham, my home for over 40 years. They're wonderful, they're warm-hearted, they're *Normal for Norfolk*, and special to me.

ISBN 978-1-916838-67-3

Cover design by Derek Blois BA(Hons)

Printed in Great Britain by
Biddles Books Limited, King's Lynn, Norfolk

# TALES FROM A COUNTRY BOY

## A Treasury of Norfolk

### Barrie Lawrence

Barrie Lawrence was born in Norfolk towards the end of the Second World War. His childhood was spent in rural locations within the county, where his fascination with wildlife led to biology being his favourite subject at school, which in turn steered him towards training to be a dental surgeon. There is obviously a longer story than that short statement might suggest. Five years training at the London Hospital (now the Royal London), and with a university degree in dentistry, and a qualification from the Royal College of Surgeons of England, he was soon back in Norfolk. His initially small practice grew, with 7 surgeries in the city and the county in his heyday. And there was his bookshop for 20 years, though he had started writing at a young age. To date, Barrie has 8 published books, selling mainly in the U.K. and North America, though one has been translated into *Farsi* and published in Iran. A strange story, for another day.

Now retired, he and Wendy enjoy a slightly more relaxed life, enjoying walking, reading, and writing, whilst spending time with their 6 daughters and 20 grandchildren, who live in 5 different countries. And, of course, Norfolk.

### Jasper MacDonald

Jasper McDonald was born in the quaint little fishing village of Dunbar, on the east coast of Scotland, where the picturesque Victorian harbour, and stunning coastline, have inspired many to take to the sketch pad or canvas. Norfolk? From early childhood, Jasper has regularly visited the county, where many family members reside.

Jasper showed talent as an artist, and particularly sketching, from an early age. Soon to be at University studying psychology, career options are quite open, though sketching will always be a part of their life. A much loved grandchild of Wendy and Barrie, they are pleased to include Jasper's sketchings in this latest volume on Norfolk.

# Preface

*Big Blue Sky* (2022) was a sort of accident. It was never meant to happen. Which reminds me of a vicar friend, who told me that he had four children, adding, "Two were accidents, and two were mistakes". *Big Blue Sky* might have been something of an accident, but when a pile of copies of the book were spotted in Waterstones, and a few other book shops and department stores in East Anglia, I felt it was not a mistake. It had spawned off from the pandemic, which had resulted in Wendy and me walking footpaths, riverbanks, and bridleways within 2 miles (and maybe a little further, at times) of our home. That, in turn, caused me to scribble. Well, tap!

'Keep yew a'troshin', said one or two local friends, who viewed several copies of the book in *Roys of Wroxham*. Now there's a Norfolk incongruity, of which the county boasts many. *Roys of Wroxham* describes itself as 'the world's largest village store'. However, *Roys* is not situated in Wroxham, but in Hoveton, which is on the northern side of the river Bure. Wroxham is on the southern side. I spent many of my childhood years in Wroxham, but one day paused and thought, 'But Roys isn't in Wroxham'. Had anyone else realised? Had 'Mr. Roy' realised? This is an example of *Normal for Norfolk*, and in general terms, just one of the reasons why I love my home county. So I started tapping away at my tablet again, and produced this companion volume. *Tales from a Country Boy - A Treasury of Norfolk,* is anecdotes, memories, a multitude of country characters, and some fascinating background facts and figures.

I hope you enjoy reading about Norfolk, as much as I have enjoyed writing about this wonderful county.

Barrie Lawrence
Frettenham, Norfolk.

January 2024

# Contents

# Sketches

*The subzero temperatures had lifted a little, and the wind dropped, as I strolled hand-in-hand with Red Legs, under a big blue sky.* 249

*As we approached our village, we were entertained by 3 fox cubs, playing together like puppies, pouncing and rolling, under the watchful eye of their vixen mother.* 265

*And when you're on a bicycle, you discover that Norfolk is not so flat, after all.* 273

*A large deer materialised out of the descending dusk, and at a leisurely pace, moved across the lawn at the top of our garden.* 275

# Introduction

"Are yer awlrite bor?" shouts Tater through his lowered driver's window, as he glides to a halt outside my cottage, seeing me clearing the ditch. He means, 'Hello my friend!' 'Are yer awlrite bor' is Norfolk for 'How are you?' I'm a 'bor' in my home county of Norfolk, as are most chaps aged from 0 to 100, or more, and indeed, ladies too. There's equality for you! I'm a country bor, with nearly 80 years of country experience. Norfolk experience. My anecdotes can keep me on my feet for an hour or more (usually less) when speaking after a dinner, or more usually, to groups such as Probus, Rotary, and the glorious Women's Institute. And I know a little local history too. I treasure my experiences of Norfolk and the wonderful people of the county who have enriched my life. Hence the title this bor has given the tome, *Tales from a Country Boy - A Treasury of Norfolk.*

There are those who might raise their eyebrows at 'another book by Barrie on Norfolk?' Well, I'm as surprised as anyone, but then, I never set out to write *any* books. I was an after-dinner speaker until Covid. I haven't been asked since – maybe there are no formal dinners since the plague. Perhaps the diners failed to sit 2 metres apart, and as a result, later expired? But, in those pre-Covid days, and quite often at such functions, I would be told, "You must write a book". And then there was our favourite patient at my county practice, the inimitable, and so sadly, late, Professor Toby Lewis. Between probing and rinses, he would encourage me, "Write a book, Barrie". After I had retired, Toby and I continued to meet up every 6 months, however, not in the surgery but in various inns and restaurants, and with that signature twinkle in his eye, he would ask, "Have you written your book yet?"

He was referring to my stories and anecdotes of 'looking down in the mouth', with which I had entertained diners for many years. So I wrote the book, and yet it was my second published. I loved my patients and my work as a dentist, but my Christian faith takes priority over all else, and my first book was of the *genre*, Religion. Simple stories of a changed life, answered prayers, and a few miracles - everyday stuff really. The book inspired by Toby was *A Dentist's Story*. Its sales exceed those of subsequent books, except for *Big Blue Sky*, and the number bought in North America is greater than those in the UK. It was also translated into *Farsi* and published in Iran. I have 2 copies, but will never read them. Those who do, start at the back, apparently.

To date I have had 8 books published, of which 3 are light, humorous, anecdotal, plus interesting facts, 3 are religious, and 2 are on my much beloved county of Norfolk. A brief description of each can be found at the back of this volume.

And then the pandemic struck, which ended much of my speaking. (Do any of my readers need a speaker to entertain?). Boris permitted us to walk, so long as we did it 2 metres distant from others. So Wendy and I walked - footpaths, bridleways, river banks, disused railway tracks, and suchlike, all in my home county of Norfolk, and usually with our village home being the start and finish. But there was a sense of *déjà vu*, as I reflected back on my teenage years, and how in the county of my birth, and just a very few miles from where I now reside, I had then walked footpaths, bridleways, river banks and disused railway tracks, catching field mice under hay bales, trapping coypu in water meadows beside the river Bure, and generally enjoying the Norfolk countryside. These pandemic perambulations resulted in this Norfolk boy, who was never going to write a book in the first place, and who had stopped forever after the first 6, scribbling again. I felt it was rather amateurish, as it's more of a hobby than a business. Grandchildren and a few friends supplied sketches. Some were not too smart, but this is Norfolk! My lovely wife, Wendy, proofread the manuscript a few times, and so did I, scores of times. One always misses something, which catches the eye next time through. Friends Jonny D'Angour and Barry Harvey also scrutinised it. I typeset the manuscript myself, and organised its printing, locally. A wholesaler gave it a look, and then took a few boxes.

"Just seen a pile of your books in Waterstones", said a friend, and known comedian. I ignored him. And then, whilst lunching at the home of good friends Bindu and Julian, I was told, "We've seen a pile of your books in Waterstones". I gave an enquiring glance across the most delicious plate of *chicken jalfrezi* and rice, plus innumerable equally delectable accompaniments, and Julian gave the widest of smiles, and said, "I took a photograph of them for you". So it was true. And since then, I have received from other friends, photographs of piles of my book, in various stores and bookshops. Perhaps it is not so flattering - do they feel it's truly amazing that decent bookshops would want to stock books by *Barrie Lawrence*? But I am grateful for the encouragement, which has resulted in a little more scribbling.

There is always more. I had felt there was insufficient material for my first Norfolk book, until I started writing. But whilst walking the footpaths, bridleways, riversides and generally meandering around the local countryside, one reflects on previous walks. Thousands of previous walks. Stories, tales, and memories from the past come to mind. And then one bumps into one of the local characters, and remembers his story of losing a cow, which others found stuck in the door of a fish and chip shop (and causing immense consternation). A week or two later, a Land Rover stops in the lane and another local legend talks of the time he moved a protesting villager's car with his fork lift truck. The result? - another book is born.

Most of our 20 grandchildren are studying much of the time, at school, college or university, though some have graduated and are working. One is actually a policeman - "Mind how you go now!" Some helped illustrate my previous book on the county, but they are all busy, busy, busy, and so I put out a few enquiries about artists. Well, people with talent, amongst our friends and family. I received an amazing response, from well over a dozen people. Wonderful, but... the first person approached only works from photographs (fair enough), the second supplied a few sketches, which were excellent, but felt she really wanted to spend her time these days on abstracts (understandable), and the third found she was too stretched between work and tending her newborn. I was about to approach the fourth, when our daughter Heather sent a Facebook message, saying that grandchild Jasper is quite handy with pencil and sketch pad. So we are keeping it in the family again, and Jasper (in Scotland - *shhh*) has used WhatsApp to supply me with some beautiful yet simple sketches to lighten up the text. Thank you Jasper.

So come and meet some of my Norfolk family, friends and quirky characters. The names, locations and descriptions of some characters, especially those who sail close to the law, and talk squit, has been changed to avoid embarrassment. I also include short items of history, and of various matters concerning the countryside, as well as describing attractions that might entertain visitors to the county. This country bor has enjoyed the county for nearly 8 decades, and invites you to indulge yourself in this treasury of Norfolk.

·

# Chapter One

## Characters

*Miss Parker's nose, the bird whisperer, Gassie's warts,*
*Mucker, and Mr. Potato*

Maud terrified me. She scared the other little children in
the village too. But there were also those characters from
my childhood where, with hindsight, I continue to
chuckle. Miss Onions and Mr. Potato, for example, not to
mention Gassie. And there are also colourful, quirky
characters from around our village, past and present;
wily, crafty countrymen, who in all their encounters with
authority, the law and the establishment, seem to come
out on top. However, Maud terrified me, and one of the
reasons was the legend of *Old Shuck*. Let me share a little
piece of spine-chilling local folklore (which some would
insist is *history*) with you.

A clap of thunder heralded the arrival of a terrifying
electric storm, and caused all in the church to catch their
breath. But that was nothing to what followed. As the
congregation knelt and prayed for mercy, the doors of St.
Mary's church flew open, and a huge black dog,
described as a Hell Hound, entered. It charged up the
nave, killing a man and a boy with its huge teeth and
deadly claws. Simultaneously, the steeple fell through the
roof, after which the dog was gone. A short time later,
the same black dog appeared in Blythburgh church, on
the coast, where it killed several more people. These
incidents were attributed to the Devil, and scorch marks
on the church doors in Blythburgh were cited as
evidence, and remain to this day. Was the dog *Black*

*Shuck*, who roams more widely in the region? Theories vary, but the incident has resulted in there being a terrifying cast-iron black dog on the weather vane in the market square in Bungay, and the creature is also incorporated in the town's coat of arms.

"So Barrie, be very careful about going out after dark, because it is said that this fearsome creature still roams dark lanes and footpaths across East Anglia". Such was the explanation proffered to my simple question, "Why are the Bungay Town football team called the Black Dogs?"

*******

I was born in Norfolk, and have spent most of my life in the county. However, the family business of over two hundred years - haberdashery, drapery and furniture – was, and continues to be, situated in the centre of the town of Bungay, which is just over the border in Suffolk. In fact, it lays along the county border, defined by the river Waveney. South of the river is Suffolk, and north is Norfolk. Where Bungay spills over that border, it is called Ditchingham. Well, that was the way it seemed to me in my younger days, though Ditchingham was, in fact, a village in its own right. The name is unusual, and it is said to be translated from old English as 'dwellers of the ditch', and although that may not be regarded as altogether flattering, the village later became famous for 'chicken roundabout' (of which more elsewhere), and of being the home of the novelist, Sir Henry Rider Haggard, author of *King Solomon's Mines*. And within the village is All Hallows' Nursing Home, which was my place of birth. I'm a Norfolk dumpling.

A few days after I was born, my mother returned to the family home in Bungay. But for the rest of my childhood, wherever we lived, which was usually in Norfolk, we were so often back in Bungay, visiting grandparents, aunts, uncles, cousins, great aunts and great uncles, and regularly watching Bungay Town football team. Eventually, following my father's retirement, my parents moved from Norfolk to Bungay, and settled amongst the wider family for their remaining years. They continued to support the town's football team, who were known as the Black Dogs, after the terrible incident in St. Mary's church on the 4th of August, 1577.

"His howling at night makes one's blood run cold, but his footfall is silent. If you *see* Black Shuck, you will be in for a dreadful time. So if you hear him, keep your eyes closed!"

Keep my eyes closed? Much better to stay indoors. With stories such as that of the terrifying black dog, and similar scary legends, fairy stories and folklore passed on to children of a young age, perhaps it is not surprising that there are times when the crazy thought, 'I wonder if there is a lion, or a bogeyman, under the bed?', or something very similar, causes them, and older ones, to prefer to have a light on at night. And with a childhood background of such stories, it is no small wonder that relatively harmless aspects of rural life could be interpreted as quite sinister.

*******

Suddenly the nursery became very dark. I froze. Whereas the bright sunshine had been pouring in through the sash window facing onto the road, it had now transformed into the silhouette of a witch. And the witch was real, and

Maud terrified me. She scared the other little children in
the village too!

pushing forward into and against the window. Furthermore, I could sense that she was staring at *me*. I broke out in a cold sweat, and my heart started pounding. I wanted to scream, but nothing came out.

The nursery door swung open. I jumped, and a little shout of alarm did come out this time. My mother stared at me, and then at the window, where the end of the witch's nose was pressed hard against the glass, and was flat and white.

"Maud! That woman is the limit". Mother shot out of the nursery, and I heard the front door open. She was raising her voice. "Maud. Maud. How dare you peer and pry like that. Get away from that window. You have frightened my little boy". And almost immediately, the sunshine was pouring back through the nursery window as the silhouette shrank quickly and moved away.

Maud was one of our village characters. There were several, and for me, aged around three or four years, she was the most scary. She was a little less than average height, dumpy, slow, and purple. Her crumpled, faded, purple-patterned ankle-length dress never changed. Maybe literally. She wore a beret, purple, and dusty. From under that beret, her rather wide, flat face stared blankly ahead. If I had been a little older, I might have described her as spooky or creepy. My mother described her as harmless.

Maud was a simple soul. I did not know where she lived in the village, or to whom she might have been related, or what she did when not shuffling slowly along the high street. But her penchant for leaning against windows, pressing her nose against the glass, and staring in was more than scary. Especially for a small curly-haired toddler, still in his pre-school years. And after in excess of seventy further years, I can still remember her clearly.

Likewise Miss Onions. There was nothing scary or creepy about Miss Onions, but she evoked my curiosity. Tall, thin, middle-aged and always by herself, she tended to dress in pale coloured clothing. She would walk with intention. She was going somewhere. She never ambled or shuffled, and she would never pause long enough to peer through a stranger's ground floor window. But she caused me to take great interest in an aspect of her facial anatomy. It was her cheeks. They looked like onions. Her face was somewhat weathered, with a degree of creasing and wrinkling. However, her cheeks were smooth and creamy, and spherical. I would stare at her, as young children do. Her cheeks reminded me of the large onions my father harvested from our back garden. Today we buy them in netting packs of two or three from supermarkets. But I would gaze at those cheeks, and in my four-year old mind, would consider, 'Her cheeks look like onions, and she is called Miss Onions. Is that why she is called Miss Onions?' Another memory from very early childhood, and one that returns from time to time, often in the vegetable department of our local supermarket.

And whilst on a vegetable theme… It was the first day of term at the primary school in the village of Wroxham. The form teacher for the year above our class had left at the end of the previous term. Who was the new teacher? What did he, or she, look like? Rumour was rife, and someone had heard that it was a man. What was his name, and what would he look like? None of our class had seen him, and we assumed he was with the big children in the class above. But next year, we would be the big children, and he would be our teacher.

And then there were excited whispers. Rita had been to the toilet, and Margaret from the class above us was there too. So now the news was out, and indeed, the whispers around our class room were extremely excited. And there was smirking, and suppressed giggling.

Rita whispered to Sandra, and Sandra whispered to Michael, who whispered to Humbo (no-one was quite sure why he was called Humbo), who sniggered behind his hand, and whispered to Paul. And Paul lent over to me.

"Mr. Potato. His name is Mr. Potato. Margaret told Rita in the toilets. Mr. Potato".

Everybody wanted to see what Mr. Potato looked like. Maybe a brownish oval face with little or no hair? We were soon to find out. All classes were to finish early that morning, and assemble together in the hall. Sitting tightly together in rows on forms, we realised that there were three new members of staff. Two were men, but which was Mr. Potato? The headmaster, Mr. Mattocks, called for silence, and explained that he wanted to introduce three new members of staff to the school. The little children in class one were to be taught by Mrs. Robinson. She stepped forward. The children in class two would have Mr. Cole as their form master. He stepped forward. And for form four... we waited with barely concealed excitement.... "I would like to introduce Mr. Tate". There was silence, of course, but I looked enquiringly at Paul, who looked at Humbo, who looked at Michael, who looked at Sandra, who looked at Rita. Rita was staring across at class four, and fixed her eye on Margaret, who grinned widely and stuck her tongue out at her.

*******

"Mummy, why does that lady have sticking plaster over the end of her nose?" One could not help but notice, and it made the lady just a little bit scary.

It was the late 1940s, and medicine and surgery had not advanced to the extent that they have today. Currently 2023. Seeing someone with a sticking plaster somewhere on their flesh would not be remarkable. Even to a four year old boy. But if that person *always* had sticking plaster in the same place, then that would beg a question. Certainly, to a four year old boy. And Miss Parker had it on her nose.

So I asked my mother why Miss Parker always had a sticking plaster on the end of her nose. Looking back, I expect that my mother had asked someone else, as we did not know Miss Parker personally. She was a late middle-aged lady, usually dressed in navy blue, who was often seen walking along the village high street. With sticking plaster over the end of her nose.

"She had something called a growth, Barrie. On the end of her nose. They cut it off in hospital, because it was growing into her face and doing her harm. Her nose doesn't look very nice now, so she wears a sticking plaster over it".

That was well over seventy years ago, but my memory of Miss Parker and her sticking plaster remains. Likewise, my mother's explanation. I was too young and well-behaved, then, to be cheeky. If I had been a few years older, I would have had an unkind nickname for the lady. To me, Miss Parker was defined by her nose!

*******

During my early teenaged years, father introduced Gassie to the family. His face was carpeted with warts. And one day we found out why.

My father worked in a local bank as a clerk. In such employment, it was usual to be moved around from branch to branch, and this indeed had been my father's experience. From Cambridge, to Royston in Hertfordshire, to Wroxham in Norfolk, and then three successive branches in Norwich, before being sent to North Walsham, around ten miles north of Norwich. North Walsham was convenient, as my sister and I were both at schools in the town. So my parents bought a house in North Walsham, and moved the family to the town. No bussing to school for my sister and me, and no driving to work for father. In fact, father's black bicycle became something of his signature, like Chamberlain's umbrella, Churchill's cigar, Maggie's handbag, and Boris' hair. "I remember your father", contemporaries of his still say to me. "Dick. He always rode a black bicycle to work".

When he was told he was being moved yet again, he said 'No'. It might have cost him his job, and certainly cost him any possible promotion, but he told them he liked Norfolk, and he loved North Walsham. Besides, he had made friends there, and such people are important. One of father's friends was Gassie. And his face was covered with warts.

Gassie was late middle-aged, of average height, and slightly stooped. Under his receding, greying hair, he wore rimless glasses. His suit - he always wore a grey suit - had seen better days. Or years. Or decades, even. I felt he looked both sad and sinister, but was sure he was harmless. Even if his face was a mass of warts.

27

"Some people collect stamps, and some collect spoons. But I collect warts", said Gassie, with a thin smile.

"Gassie's coming round this evening", mother would say, "So stay out of the dining room, because your father is helping him with his books". His books? - accounts, receipts, financial and trading records, and the like. Mr. Gasgoine was his real name, and he was a small retailer in the town. It was mutually beneficial for him to visit father once a month to 'do the books'. For father, it was a little work on the side, earning extra money, of which part might even have been in cash. For Gassie, as my mother, and therefore Julia and I, called him (in his absence), it meant that he did not need to engage the services of an accountant, which would have been much more expensive. But why did he have so many warts?

"Do stay for a cup of tea, Mr. Gasgoine", said my mother in the hallway, and a couple of minutes later, he shuffled into the sitting room and made himself comfortable in an armchair. Julia and I tried not to stare, but at our young age, it was very difficult. And there were so many warts.

"Been a nice day", said Gassie, as mother brought a cup of tea through. "Thank you for the tea, and I am grateful to Dick for looking after my accounts". And looking towards Julia and I, "Have you two had a good day?"

We muttered a few words about school, which wasn't really too bad. And we tried not to stare at his warts.

"Do you like my warts?" ventured Gassie. We looked at him blankly and a little embarrassed, not knowing how to answer. "I've collected them over the years, I have. Some people collect stamps, and some people collect spoons. But I collect warts". He gave a thin smile, and added, "But I'm embarrassing you. I'll explain". Now he had us curious, and he had our attention.

"It runs in the family, you see. Not having warts, but *collecting* warts. My father collected them, and his father before him. They're not really *our* warts - they're other peoples'. Some people like to say they hope to leave this world a better place. You know, when they go. Well, when I go, pass on like, I'll leave it a less warty place". Thin smile again. "Cos I'll be taking other people's warts out of this world. Got any warts, either of you?"

"Julia's got a wart", said mother. "She's put those wart-removing ointments on it, but there's no change. It's quite stubborn. So what can you do about it, Mr. Gasgoine?"

"I'll buy it from you", said Gassie. " I'll give you a penny for it, which means it's mine after that. And in a few days, you'll find it's gone. And I'll have another wart". Another weak smile. "Would you like that?"

"Nothing to lose", mother said to Julia, "And even if the wart doesn't go, you'll be a penny better off".

So Gassie put his hand in his pocket, and pulled out a selection of small change. He found a penny, and handing it to Julia, said, "I now buy your wart. It's mine". Julia took the penny and placed it on the table beside her chair. "My father used to pay people a ha'penny, and my grandfather paid people a farthing. Inflation!" He gave a small cough. Or was it a laugh?

A week later at breakfast, my sister said, "Guess what. My wart has gone".

Three weeks later, Gassie was back with his books. "Julia's wart has gone", mother told him.
"I know", he said. "It's on the back of my neck".

It sounded spooky to me, and from then on, I gave him a wide berth. Today, I would consider it occult, and give him a wider berth. But one had to admit that Gassie left this world a less warty place.

*******

"W' blust. If yew want muck, Oi'm yer man. Mucker by name, and mucker by trade", said the plump, rosy cheeked, wild-haired man standing on our doorstep.

It was well over 40 years ago when I moved into my quaint little country cottage in the village of Frettenham. Our local post-master Eric, had suggested I use the board for postcard ads in his village grocery store cum post office cum stationer's cum information bureau. And all within the space of what had once been the front room of Eric's home. I had been chatting about the quality of the soil in my garden, and Eric had taken off his postman's cap, and donned that of chief information officer. Then he had a better idea.

"Yew can put a postcard on my advertising board. *WANTED - MUCK*! yew could write. And yer name and phone number. But yew need to see Mucker", said Eric. "He'll git yer some 'orse muck, he will. 'E keeps 'orses. And cows. And sheep. 'E often droives through the village with a trailer full o' muck. Smell 'im for hours, yew can. Oi'll give yew 'is number. Of course, Mucker ain't his real name. 'E's Moike really. Moichal 'Ickling. But 'e goes by Mucker. Always 'as".

And Michael Hickling, aka Mike, but usually known as Mucker, was an integral and much-loved character in our village. Of average height, above average girth, and with eyes that twinkled with unabated *joie de vivre*, he had a smile and a story for everyone. He was an open-air countryman, with those ruddy cheeks and untamed hair, that could almost be described as feral.

"W' blust, Oi can't read and Oi can't wroite, but yew ring me or leave me a message. If Oi git a message, Oi ring them and ask who they are. Eric said yew want muck. Oi'll bring yew muck when Oi bring my next lood through the village", he said with a twinkle. But not being able to write meant there was little point in having a diary. Sometimes Mucker's memory worked, and this time it did not. But the soil had produced good vegetables for the previous owner, and did likewise for me for two or three years. Then I ploughed up the kitchen garden, doubled the area of lawn, and used a greenhouse for tomatoes, cucumbers and the like. And from then on, no muck was required.

Mucker was Norfolk through and through. Born in the county, he had never lived more than ten miles from his place of birth. He was a collection of contradictions. On the one hand, he was the quintessential country bumpkin, and yet, he was as sharp as a razor. He would give a silly grin and plead poverty, and yet could produce a few hundred thousand pounds *in cash* to buy a property at virtually no notice.

"He's a crafty man", said my friend John, former resident of the village, and now living a few miles distant in our nearest town. "He is the crafty son of a crafty father, who was in turn a crafty son of a crafty father. Three generations of crafty people. Now they've all passed on, except Mucker, and he is all alone. No relations, but a collection of farms. All left to him by family".

"But some years ago, they were all alive and living in the village. Well, they also had somewhere in Brunton, and another place in Harsford. All really close to here. But they were a crafty lot", continued John. "Mucker's real name is Michael Hickling. His father's name was Michael Hickling. And his grandfather's name was Michael Hickling. Well, they were always wheeling and dealing, and sometimes they would start building some sort of extension or annex to their home, or be putting up some new storehouse or workshop on their land, to accommodate their latest business equipment, or whatever they were selling. No planning permission - they just built. And then some bloke from the council would turn up and read the riot act. He would say, 'Are you Michael Hickling?' And if it was Mucker, he would say, 'Michael Hickling is my grandad. You need to see him'. And if it was his father or grandfather when the council came round, they would say, 'Michael Hickling is my son. You need to see him', or 'Michael Hickling is my father. You need to see him'. The council chaps would get really angry, but the Hicklings would just stare at them. Act dumb. Real cool. Then the council bloke would clear off. After a while, the extension would come down 'cos they didn't need it anymore. Then, after a year or so, they would build another one, and the council would go through the whole procedure again. Now there's just Mucker left, who can't read or write, but with at least three properties and several farms. Crafty people, they were".

That was around forty years ago when I first came to the village. Mucker was quite a character, to put it mildly, and the stories continue. He and his family could almost be described as legends; we continue to laugh at the stories, and maybe future generations will enjoy them too.

And then there was Digger, whose real name was unknown to me. Everyone seemed to know the man, whose name aptly described his physique, though there was some debate as to where he actually resided. 'Out Brunton way', was probably as near as one got to accuracy, and 'in a bit of a shack, that used to be a farmhouse' might well have described his home. Like Mucker, he had a somewhat ambivalent attitude to the law, and on at least one occasion, his dealing with the police was confrontational. Driving through our local city of Norwich, towing a livestock trailer containing a cow and its calf, Digger was pulled over by a police car.

"You might need to polish up your driving skills, but I think you've got far too much in your trailer", said the officer. Or words to that effect. And so Digger was instructed to follow the police car to a nearby weighbridge. (A weighbridge is a device for weighing vehicles, set into the ground so that the vehicle can be driven onto it.)

"W'll blust!" Digger told me, "Oi driv onto the weighbridge, disconnected the trailer and left it sitting there. So this carpper messes around with switches and stuff, and then comes oover and tells me moi trailer is too heavy. So Oi tell him, 'Oi'll make it loighter then', and I opened the doors on the back of the trailer, and the cow and calf jumped out and went charging round his yard. You should have seen his face. Dead scared. He got behind some railings and said, 'Yew'll have to sort this out'. So Oi tell him, 'Oi've made the trailer loighter. Yew can sort your yard out. That's *your* jarb".

Digger continued with intermittent chuckles, enthusing over reliving the experience, where he knew that he had the upper hand.

"So he say to me, 'I don't know nothing about cows', and I told him he better larn quick afore they did some damage. Then he say to me, 'What do *yew* know about cows?', and so I tell him, 'They gart four legs, and they shit. So watch out'. He didn't think that was very funny, and told me to get them back in the trailer and clear orf. So that's what Oi did. What a larf, eh?"

*******

"My husband's a shepherd, aren't you Freddie? He knows absolutely *everything* about the countryside. All the little creatures that scurry around, and trees and flowers, don't you Freddie? He is so knowledgeable. And every bird - he can tell you all about them. Can't you Freddie? He's a shepherd, you see".

Freddie didn't utter a word. Not even a faint bleat. Marie didn't seem to notice, and continued to extol the virtues of her husband, while his slightly diminutive form sat limply beside her on our sitting room sofa.

We had known Marie years earlier, when we were members of the same church. We had moved, and so had she. And then she had met Freddie, fallen in love, and the rest was history. And now we had met up again. She was a strong personality, an academic and professionally qualified. Freddie was a shepherd, small of stature, weatherbeaten, and virtually silent. I volunteered that I would love to have just a fraction of Freddie's obvious encyclopaedic knowledge of the British countryside, and especially since living in such a rural location.

"Did you hear that, Freddie? Barrie would love to learn about the countryside, and all the plants and trees and flowers and bugs and birds…"

"Did you hear that, Freddie? Barrie would like to learn about the countryside", said Marie.

I interrupted to say that there was a limit to how much information I could absorb, and I thought that if Freddie could teach me just a little about birds, that would be wonderful.

"Do yer walk?" asked the shepherd quietly. "We can walk from hair, at yer home hair. One day next week, if yer loike?"

You bet! And so we arranged it for the following Monday. I'd pick him up. Drive him over. Walk along footpaths, across fields, by a stream and through woods to the *White Horse* pub restaurant. Have lunch and return. I couldn't wait.

The day duly arrived, and found me clad in green trousers and waterproof jacket. And a green hat. If I looked like a tree, the birds might come closer. Freddie wore blue jeans and a red checked shirt. There was minimal conversation.

We walked through the village, and had covered, perhaps, 50 yards, when Freddie broke the silence.

"*Shhh*", he whispered. "There's a greenfinch in the top of the tree on the right opposite. I'll talk to it and ask it to come down".
"What!" I exclaimed, amazed. "*Shhh*", said Freddie, with a gentle hint of rebuke. And he started making birdlike whistling noises, with one eye on the tree. The bird responded with some tweets, after which Freddie made some more muted whistles.
"He's coming down", he whispered, and sure enough, the greenfinch left its high perch and swooped down, into a small bush about 6 feet away to our left. Freddie

twittered and tweeted, and the bird tweeted back. And again.

"He's not coming any closer because he's too scared. Too careful, I should say. Let's carry on". And leaving the bird in the bush, Freddie continued along Post Office Road in the direction of the footpath.

He pointed out a few other birds on the way. I wish I could remember them. But it was a fascinating and interesting time. However, the best was yet to come. As we approached the hamlet of Crostwick, crossing a bridge over a brook, where my children used to play Pooh sticks, there are dense bushes, like brushwood, lining the western side of the B1150. These would have formed a barrier for us, but a tunnel of around 15 feet in length, and maybe 7 feet high and wide, had been cut through, and enabled walkers to reach the road, cross it and stroll down to the *White Horse* pub restaurant. We were halfway through the tunnel when there was an invasion of small birds. Their movement was rapid, and we were surrounded by tweeting and squeaking. Quite remarkably, they were weaving their way through the seemingly impenetrable brushwood. Freddie stopped, and gave me another '*Shhh*'. Then he began tweeting, and when he did so, the birds seemed to stop. Then Freddie became quiet, and the birds started again. Then Freddie, and then the birds. And then again. "We can move on", he whispered. "That's all for now".

"What was all that about?" I enquired. "Were you really talking to them?"

"Of course", he replied. "But they are off for lunch, and will be back in about an hour and a half".

"Shhh", Freddie whispered. "There's a greenfinch. I'll talk
to it and ask it to come down".

I was flabbergasted. Surely Doctor Dolittle was a fictional character, but here was Freddie, in Norfolk in the 21st century, having a conversation with birds, who told him they were 'off for lunch, and will be back in an hour and a half'. This man was a genuine bird-whisperer! At times I am so naïve. With genuine amazement, I stammered, 'They told you *that*?"

I had not seen Freddie smile before, but surely there was just the hint of one for around a second or two. "No", he said, and went on to explain. "We can't understand each other, but they stop to listen because I can do bird calls and sounds. And I know their habits, feeding times, routines and such like. These birds fly north, usually through vegetation, feeding all the way. When the sun is at its highest, they turn round and fly south back to their roost. I can tell from the sun's position, that they have around another 45 minutes before they turn. So, back in an hour and a half, all the while having lunch. I don't really converse with them, but I know what they do. I've watched them all my life".

I felt so silly, but also impressed with Freddie's obvious skill, knowledge and understanding of the countryside. It was a memorable day, and though we said we would do it again, his memory was starting to deteriorate, and a few years later, he needed to be in a residential home. I sometimes try and recall what the birds were, but my memory is deteriorating too. Were they goldcrests, or is that too rare a species to visit Crostwick? And I really wish this remarkable man well in his latter, retirement years, and trust there will be other Norfolk shepherds, or simple countrymen, who enjoy this amazing creation, and who can inspire the likes of me with their knowledge.

*********

Tater became a sort of friend. I think he used to be known for planting and harvesting potatoes. The potato king. Tater! But by the time I knew him, he had diversified. If I was strimming the bank by our back door, or digging the ditch, or hedging along the lane, a brand spanking new Mercedes pick-up, occasionally towing a trailer full of potatoes, would draw up. Tater would turn the engine off, give me a huge smile, and say slowly, "Are yer awlroight?" The ensuing conversation invariably followed the same pattern. What was I up to? Was I alright? How was my wife? Was she alright? Did I need any help with my bank, or ditch, or hedge? He would give me a good price. Further smiles, grins and twinkles. Once I asked him to reshingle my drive. Mistake. A truck dumped a mountain of pebbles onto my drive, and Tater and a mate appeared with rakes. It cost several times the estimate ('But it'll last yew fer yairs') and my wife and I felt we were at least ankle deep in shingle ('W' blust. Oi'll give yew credit on it fer next toime.'). There was no next time, but Tater continued as my friend, often stopping to tell me of his most recent adventure.

"Did yer hair about moi larst cow?" Mercedes parked in the lane, blocking any traffic that might appear. Engine off. Tater grinning.

"W' blust", he continued. "Oi gart a lart of pasture around Brunton. Have yer walked the footpath from Marnham to Brunton?" I nodded. "W'll, that's all mine", he said. "Both sides of the river". He paused. "Have yer walked the footpath from Brunton to Cowdon?", he continued. I started to get the picture, and said that my

41

wife and I knew the footpath well. "All mine. Both sides of the river". Yes, I had got the picture.

"So I move the cows", he said. Did that cheeky grin ever fade? "Well, there was only ten, and Oi was walking them through Brunton village. And blust, one of the beggars made a run for it". (Well, Tater did not actually say 'beggars'; it sounded a bit like it, but let's be polite and pretend he did.) "So Oi'm not garnna leave noine. W' blust, they would cause chaos. So I took 'em off to the medder darn Cowdon way, when moi phone rung. 'Hev yew larst a cow?' someone asked. 'Cos there's a cow stuck in the door of the fish and chip sharp in the village, and a lartta people are getting upset'. Noo prarblem. Only a cow. Soo I goo and get it out. Women shouting, and some kids crying and some kids laughing. Noo big deal. Oonly a cow".

Reflecting upon Tater's stories always makes me smile. But let me share a few stories concerning another old Norfolk countryman. And in case you, the reader, are from outside this county, I will revert to normal English. But that is not the way Mucker, Digger, Tater, or Tad spoke.

Tad was a middle-aged wiry man, with a prematurely wrinkled face due to years of sun, wind, rain and everything else the Norfolk elements had thrown at him during his 50 or so years. "I wish I could read and write like some people can", he said with that engaging grin. "I expect you can read and write. I sometimes have a go, but it just doesn't work for me. I thought I'd have a few sheep, but I had to write down how many I wanted. I thought a hundred and twenty would be good. But guess what? - I got over a thousand. I told them I'd ordered a hundred and twenty, and where did all these come from?" Tad was still grinning at me, so I guessed it was no disaster. "Do you know what I done? I'd put too many noughts on. Got twelve hundred instead of a hundred and twenty".

I asked what he did with so many sheep. Could they be sent back? He shrugged his shoulders and laughed. "I've got plenty of land. Lots of grass. So I put the sheep out there. No problem. But I'll get someone else to fill the form in next time".

And another anecdote from Tad. "I was working on my farm one day when this bloke drove up and parked his car across the entrance. I just thought he'd stopped to buy something, but then I recognised him. His brother Harry had done some work for me, and Harry is alright. But Denis, the brother who'd parked his car across my entrance, was a load of trouble.

'You owe my brother money, and I've come for it', said Denis.
'Well, I'm not giving it to you', I said. 'I'll give it to Harry, but not to you'. He started shouting, and said Harry had sent him. I didn't believe him, and told him to clear off.

'I'm waiting here until I get the money', he said. 'And I'm not moving my car until I get it. So *you* won't be going anywhere'.

So I said nothing, but just turned and walked back down my drive. Denis shouted that he wasn't going to move his car until I gave him the money. I shouted, '*I'll* move it for you then'. He hollered out that it was locked, and then 'Hard luck'.

I thought, 'I'll give him hard luck!' And you should have seen his face when I drove down the drive in my fork-lift truck. And when I stuck the prongs under his car and started lifting it, he was shouting and screaming at me. Couldn't hear a word, but he was dancing and shouting at me. Got his mobile out and started yelling into it.

I dumped his car down beside the road, and told him to get the hell out of it, afore I put it somewhere he wouldn't like. So he tell me that he'd called the police. Then he swore, jumped back into his car, and was gone. And when the police come, and I tell them that Denis had been round here demanding money, they say they wanted to speak to him about another matter, and that was why he had cleared off. Didn't see him again. Good riddance".

*******

Our village has an Ian. Every village should have an Ian. A town might need 2 or 3 Ians. In fact, if you have not got an Ian, there will be times when you will be in trouble.

"Oi can mend anything. Anything at all. Bring it hair, moi man, and Oi'll fix it".

I understood that there was this chap working from a glorified shed, at the back of a site which used to be a garden centre. He was the man, I was told in the village, to service my lawn mower. He wouldn't charge too much, and it would go like a train when he had done it.

"Cors Oi can do it, moi man", he enthused. Behind him, I could see the aforementioned shed. It appeared to be packed with machinery, tools, drills, mower parts, gardening implements, and all things mechanical. In front of the shed, was a small yard, and anything for which there was no room inside, was outside. The yard was full. And in front of the yard was Ian. Average height and average girth, and muscular. Fit. Strong. His overall smeared with oil. His hands coated with more oil. Twinkling eyes under greying, bushy hair. My new friend.

I returned a week later. "It's done", said the amazing Mr. Fixit. "It's serviced for yew, but Oi've done a few adjustments too. Little gadget on the tarp hair. Flick it hair. See - yew can keep yer engine running whoil yew empty the grass frarm the box". And the cost was modest. I understood he was also a mine of information on all matters horticultural, mechanical, engineering - and possibly arboreal, I mused.

"Can you recommend someone to fell a tree for me, Ian?" I asked. "It's quite old, is swaying in a precarious manner, and threatens my greenhouse. One storm, and my lawn will be covered with shattered glass and fallen tree".

"Are yew in this evening?" asked Superman. "Cos if yew are, Oi'll call in on moi way home. Soon take a tree down".

And sure enough, early evening, a white van turned in through my gateway and parked on the drive.

"Ladder?" was the request. I fetched a ladder.

"Stand back". A chainsaw started roaring away around 15 feet above the ground.

"Catch!" - and a small section of tree trunk and branch fell to the ground at my feet with a thud.

"Butter fingers. Stand back". And another foot or three landed on the lawn. I brought the barrow over, and wheeled the sections of tree out through the gate and into the wood across the lane, where there had once been a gravel pit. Was it really ok to dump my garden waste in the pit? The owner of the wood, and disused gravel pit, was another friendly villager. "So long as it's biodegradable", I was told. So lawn cuttings, leaves, and tree parts vanished into the nether regions of the pit. But where did Henry the Hoover come from? Fly tipping is an increasing problem in our county, and probably others, and someone had craftily deposited their old vacuum cleaner alongside my earlier grass cuttings.

Within 45 minutes, there was no tree! Many sections had landed on the bed of grass, leaves, garden weeds and rose prunings in the pit, after which Ian wrestled with the stump. Push. Pull. Groan. Shove. Heave. And crash - that was the end of the tree. The cost?

"That's all roight, moi man", said our handy-man *extraordinaire*. "Moi pleasure. Noo prarblem. See yew sometime soon". And he was gone.

The wheelbarrow was so useful around my Norfolk country garden; mown grass, weeds, rose cuttings, clippings from here and snippings from there, until -

"My wheelbarrow's got a flat tyre", I told Wendy. "And it's not a weedy little tyre, but more like it belongs on a car".
"Ian!" said Wendy.

Maybe it would have fitted in the back of her estate car, but Ian was less than 1,000 yards away. So I wheeled it along the lane, bump, bump, bump past the junction, and along to the shed that some might say resembled Aladdin's Cave. Or Steptoe's yard.

"Hello moi man", was the usual greeting. I explained my predicament, and in no time, the wheel was off the barrow. Then the outer tyre was off the tube. Ian is strong, and maybe the strongest man I know. Wendy and I can take one end each of the lawn mower, and lift it into her car. Just. But Ian can tuck it under one arm, and walk across the yard with it. And then he had the inner tube to his mouth, and was blowing it up as though it was a balloon at Christmas.

"Wait yew hair. It'll be about 10 minutes", said the amazing Ian. The inner tube was fully inflated, orally. Then plunged under water, as in mending a bicycle tyre. Everything seemed to happen so fast. A cloth to dry it. A powder to desiccate it. Adhesive. Patch. Tube back in outer tyre. Tyre on wheel, and wheel on barrow. Amazing.

"Call it a foiver". I called it ten. It was worth twenty. And three years later, it's still going strong.

Shortly after that, Wendy and I had one of those repeat conversations. We had been there before, and it was rather like a record becoming stuck in a groove.

"You know how we have talked before about having electricity in the summerhouse, so that we can have light and heat there – I think we ought to do it, because we've talked about it for a few years now".

I was out when the electrician arrived, and Wendy took him to the summerhouse, and showed him the nearby outdoor socket. He started measuring, and pacing, and making notes. As he was finishing, I arrived back home, and left my car on the drive as I walked up the lawn to introduce myself. We exchanged pleasantries, and as he appeared to have finished making notes and calculations, I asked him what the cost would be.

I am sure I saw him look at my car. He stared at it. He looked back into his notebook for a minute or so, as though having a rethink. I think he did, and then said, £800". I almost gasped. A few feet of cable. A socket. Half an hour's digging. I thanked him for coming, and told him I would be in touch if I wanted him to proceed.

Problem – I drive a Bentley. It's not new enough to be worth much, and it's not old enough to be worth much. I bought it 4th hand for the price of a more modest younger car, and after 9 years, it has proved reliable, even though I have put another 100,000 miles on the clock. But it can cause electricians to raise their estimates. And then I thought of a man in the village who could mend anything, fix anything, fell trees, service mowers. I worded my enquiry carefully.

"I'm not expecting you to say *you* can do this, but do you know anyone who can take electricity up to our summer house, and fit a socket there?" I asked Mr. Fixit.

"Leave it to me. Oi'll bring some armour-plated cable round. And Oi'll bury it, and Oi'll fit yew a sarcket". And at the time of writing, the cable has been buried deeply under the lawn, and at the back of the summerhouse sits an electric log-effect fire and a table light. I had arrived back from a shopping trip to receive the cheery greeting, "All done, moi man". The cost? "Call it 50 quid – the cable is expensive stuff, but Oi had some left over from another jarb, you see".

Every village should have an Ian!

*******

Every village should have a Tony. Brunton has a Tony, but that's only 12 minutes' drive away, and so we share him. And with Cowdon, because the villages are small and Tony works all hours. A town might need 2 or 3 Tonys.

"I don't know his address", says Tater, "but Brunton is only one street, and if you look for a driveway with 3 rusty Land Rovers, piles of bricks, rubble, pipes, roofing felt, fence panels and so on, you've found him. I bet the neighbours love him!"

If you would like an extension on your house, or your gutters replaced, or your chimney repointed, Tony is the man. And should you want your ditch cleared out, he can arrange it. Or your Christmas lights hung around the gable ends of your property, then Tony is the man to call. He might even feed your chickens while you're on holiday. He did mine once.

He also knows everybody in our village, and in most other local villages too. And their parents and uncles and aunts. And whether you need a hairdresser, farrier, chiropodist, grave-digger, rat-catcher, blacksmith, swan-marker, alchemist, or whatever, Tony either knows one, or where you can find one.

Tony also knows the history of every house in the village, and in most other local villages. Some were used hundreds of years ago in cottage industries, often associated with the Flemish weavers or the Scottish drovers. And more recently, where the hairdresser, electrician, plumber, carpenter, mole man, and so many others currently live. "Just bang on their front door, and mention my name…"

I love Tony's Land Rover, which reminds me of a car driven by one of my daughters, when she worked in Bosnia just after the last Balkan war. I had been staying with her, and we visited a refugee camp one evening. She used to take the people there bread, rice, milk, and anything else she felt they needed. But there is always someone who likes to cause a bit of trouble, and one night we left the camp to find her car tyres had been slashed. We called a taxi, and returned for the car next morning. She took it to a sort of garage, where they did a sort of repair, placing a sort of Bosnian Elastoplast on the tyres, after which we drove 4 hours to Dubrovnik. "Most cars are held together with elastic bands and sellotape out here", she explained. And Tony's Land Rover reminds me of my daughter's car, with the bonnet held down with elastic bunjee straps, vibrating amidst the general rattling and banging from the vehicle. I enquired about the straps.

"Old engine conked out. No more good. But not really worth a new one. So I got one secondhand, but it doesn't fit properly. Not quite. It works alright, but it's too big, so I can't shut the bonnet. Anyway, the straps hold it down ok, and I know a bloke who does MOTs……"

Every village should have a Tony.

*******

"You live in Horse Carrot Village, do you?", said a grinning fellow member of the *Wensum Valley Golf Club*. 'Do you live locally?' is one of those ice-breaking introductory questions when meeting people at social functions - or on the golf course. At my age, 'What do you do for a living?' is deemed unnecessary. Maybe 'What *did* you do for a living?' could be seen as appropriate. But my response to the usual question brought the allusion to a large sign, seen on entering the village from a lane that leads from the main Norwich road, *HORSE CARROTS FOR SALE.* Everybody sees it. And if you see it often enough, you stop thinking too much about it. "What exactly are 'horse carrots'?", was one of those rhetorical questions that Wendy and I had asked ourselves. And then we found out.

Walking around our village not only keeps one fit, but also keeps one informed. It was early evening, and I was strolling past the horse carrots sign, which stood on top of some shelving. You can guess what was displayed for sale on the shelving, beside a hinged box with *Money* written on the side. There was a short drive leading to the entrance to a small field, or large garden, with cast iron gates. And about to close the gates was a young middle-aged fellow, with a robust outdoor appearance - jeans with soil, tartan shirt with stains, ruddy cheeks and an immediate smile.

"Are yer alright, bor?" was the customary greeting.
"Yes. You?" I replied. He was.

"Nice to meet you. I won't introduce myself by my proper name, cos no-one uses them round here. Well, none of my mates. Like Tony - but his real name is Mark. And there's Chitty, but that ain't his real name, which is Michael. So a lot of people call me Carrot, and most folk call me Worzel. I'll answer to either, but you can call me Worzel".

Worzel and I became friends immediately. Like everyone else did with Worzel. He had a small-holding where he grew mainly carrots. He also had a number of fields, where he grew carrots. Thousands and thousands of carrots. I asked how he sold so many, and he pointed to the animal sanctuary along the lane, and said, "Trailer loads!"

"And the horse carrots? Are they a special variety grown for horses?"
"No. Not special. Ordinary carrots", he answered, causing me to ask why he advertised them as 'horse carrots'.

"Cos I haven't got them qualified for human consumption", he replied. "So I call them horse carrots, and then I can't be accused of selling them for people to eat". Grin.
"So people with horses buy the carrots?"
"No. People like you and me buy them", was the reply. Big grin.
"And what do they use them for? What do they do with them?" I asked, innocently.
"They boil them up and eat them!" Big wide smile, eyes twinkling. "It's the government that has me call them horse carrots, cos I mustn't sell them for people, cos my carrots haven't got qualified. But everyone knows they're just carrots. So they get them a bit cheap, enjoy them, I ask no questions, and everybody wins, so to speak".

"*Worzel's Carrots* is my business name, though it wasn't that when I started. I was supplying hay and carrots, so I called it *Dobbin's Bed and Breakfast*. Like, horses are called Dobbin, and I was supplying hay for their bed and carrots for their breakfast. That went well, until someone got the wrong idea. I got a phone call, and thought this chap was wanting hay and carrots, but he and another chap, in suits and with brief cases, arrived by taxi, banged on my door and said they had come for bed and breakfast. Big misunderstanding! So what did I do with them, cos the taxi had gone, and it was dark? I had to phone round till I got them bed and breakfast. *The White Horse* at Crostwick took them in, so I ran them down there. Thought I'd better change the name before more people arrived asking for bed and breakfast, so now it's *Worzel's Carrots*".

I remarked that village people must be very honest, with a hinged box with no lock sitting on the shelf with money in it.

"They are now", said Worzel. "Weren't always. Someone wasn't. So I stuck some terminals in it, and a battery behind the shelves. Put the money in - no problem. Put your whole hand in to take money out, and 'Yeeeoooowwwww!' I knew when the beggar (well, he did not say beggar, but something very close) used to come, and I hid behind the hedge, and heard him yell. Blust, he yelled loud, and jumped up and down. Could have heard him in Norwich! After that I took the terminals out, and no more money's gone since. Would you like some carrots? Here - have a bag on me".

The horse carrots sign has been there for years, and Worzel has been a much-loved Norfolk character for a long time too. In Norfolk, he's called a 'good ole bor'. He's always got time for a friendly conversation, and generous with his carrots. But don't stick your hand in his box to steal his money, or you might get stung quite badly. Just a little warning, in case you ever visit Horse Carrot village and get tempted.

*******

Norfolk characters. This Norfolk bor has known a few, but one wonders whether they will weather the changes of the 21st century. There are so many people moving from the Home Counties into East Anglia, working from home or commuting to London, or simply retiring and enjoying a quieter more relaxed rural life.

I remember an article in one of our national newspapers. It was a feature article, written largely to entertain, I believe. It was about life in Norfolk, where country bumpkins abounded. We were portrayed as simple, straw chewing folk. The writer went on to mention some villages just to the south-east of Kings Lynn. According to the article, there had been so much inbreeding, and for so many generations, that many of those central to community life there had six fingers on each hand. Life in these rural villages was described as quite incestuous, with the insinuation being that the countryfolk living there were generally dull-witted puddings, who knew little of life outside the village.

Life was uncomplicated and undemanding when I was young. Maud would wander aimlessly through the village, and being simple, would press her nose against windows of cottages on the High Street, and stare in. Today, she would spend much of her time at home sitting in front of the television.

Miss Parker was unconcerned (so it seemed) that children might stare at sticking plaster on her nose. She could have stayed at home. Today, she would have had plastic surgery, and no-one would have given her a second look.

The rural rogues, and characters who lived by their wits, and made thousands of pounds regularly on deals, will be few and far between in a generation or so. Literacy increases. Forms, checks, protocols, licences, accreditations, the Internet - not everyone will achieve or comply, but the drift is away from the loveable illiterate rogues.

In a previous volume, I mentioned the jobbing gardener from my childhood, Charlie, who married the cleaner from our school. They honeymooned in Kings Lynn, and talked of that faraway place where the people spoke differently and where the weather was colder, for the rest of their lives. Charlie, Tad, Tater, Mucker, Worzel and so many others are colourful characters from a generation that is fading away, and their passing will be a loss to Norfolk country life.

# Chapter Two

## Dialect

*Pollywiggles, pishamires, barneypigs and mingins*

"There's parllywiggles acrorst the field through the wood" said Sludge. "Let's goo and get some". (And, of course, the word is not parllywiggles, which is Norfolk, but pollywiggles, which is English. Maybe you knew that, but some might be a little confused by the word. Now I'll continue).

"Hev yew got suffun what we can put 'em in?" asked Gully.

"My mum's given me a gret big jar what she had jam in'" said Stalky. "Oi reckon we can get loods on 'em in it".

And so we set off in search of the pollywiggles. Sludge said he'd seen them. Thousands. Or perhaps, hundreds. Well, he was sure there were *lots* of pollywiggles across the field through the wood.

I had read about these creatures, and some of my mates had caught a few and taken them home. But somehow, I had always missed out. Too late, or gone to the wrong place, or been given misinformation. I really wanted to catch some pollywiggles, and surely this time I would be successful. Sludge seemed so sure.

I too had a jar. Not so large as Stalky's, but big enough. If they were small pollywiggles, there would be room for a dozen. Or a few more. But I knew they came in various sizes, and were quite small when they first hatched.

We cycled out of town, and trudged over the field Sludge had alluded to in the earlier conversation. We each had a butterfly net, and there were jars of various sizes. Eventually we came to the pond, and stared into it. The reflected sky tended to obscure all detail below the surface, but at least two of us had encountered this problem before. The answer was simple; you laid on your tummy, sticking your head out beyond the water's edge, and gazed down through your own shadow.

"*Parllywiggle!*" whispered Stalky, whose long lean frame extended significantly further out over the pond than the rest of us. There was an excited scramble to get alongside Stalky. "*Shhhh*", said the man of the moment, and whispered, "Keep yer voice down, and move real slow. They've already seen yer and clared orf. Doon't move. Just wait and keep yer oyes skinned".

And so we waited, and before long, a pollywiggle came into view. There was a leisurely wiggle or two, until Gully coughed. And twitched with it. Wiggle, wiggle, wiggle - and it was gone again.

But the morning was productive, and our silent wait by the water's edge was rewarded. We each caught a few, and my own jam jar contained nine jet black pollywiggles. In the light of the sun through the glass, they were almost glossy, as I gazed and gazed, practically mesmerised by their enchanting wiggling.

You laid on your tummy, sticking your head out beyond the water's edge, and gazed down through your own shadow.

Back home in my bedroom, I had a goldfish bowl ready and waiting, and even my parents were fascinated as they stared at these amazing little creatures.

Pollywiggles need to eat, in order to grow. They are herbivores, and in the wild will eat pond weeds of various types. I had brought a small bagful home, and popped a little into the bowl each morning. They grew. Well, most of them did, but three died and were removed and buried. Buried? I was a schoolboy, and even pollywiggles got a decent burial in my father's vegetable garden. Gully told me he was feeding his on goldfish food, and so I visited the pet shop and started putting flakes of fish food into the water each morning. They grew faster, it seemed. And then, almost magically, little arms, (or were they legs?) started developing just back from their heads. This was progress indeed, and sensing that further changes were imminent, I found a large Norfolk flint, and placed it in the centre of the bowl, with at least one third protruding above the water.

My premonitions were correct, and a few days later, I returned from school one afternoon to find that the journey was over. There on the flint, in the centre of the bowl, sat the first two mature pollywiggles. They no longer had gills, but nostrils. And four legs. Once more, I was mesmerised, as I gazed at the cutest, most beautiful little frogs, you could possibly imagine.

*******

It is said that the Norfolk dialect is quite distinct, and only found within the county. But there is a curious exception, involving Gorleston-on-sea, usually referred to simply as Gorleston. Until 1832, it had been part of Suffolk, being on the west bank of the river Yare. Then, for electoral purposes, it became part of Great Yarmouth. Three years later, it became part of the borough of Great Yarmouth, and therefore Norfolk, and there are those who say that to this day, the people of Gorleston-on-sea speak the Suffolk dialect, and not Norfolk. "Blust. They're loike fareigners".

A local or regional accent refers to the pronunciation of words, whereas a dialect includes the vocabulary, spelling and grammar as well. As a lad growing up in the county, my friends and I were quite bemused by dialects from other parts of the U.K. and drawing an imaginary line from the Bristol Channel to the Wash, described those on the other side as coming from 'up north' and 'speaking funny'. I believe that view is still held by many of my fellow Norfolk people today. We felt that all Londoners sounded like cockneys, including people from Essex, as though they had leaked out through the north-eastern border of the M25, which did not exist then. And with another sweeping generalization, we were convinced that all characters from south-western England spoke like *Worzel Gummidge*. (Worzel Gummidge was a scarecrow created by Barbara Euphan Todd in her childrens' books, and made famous by the eponymous television series, starring Jon Pertwee, speaking with a heavy West Country accent). But as the years pass, one comes to recognise differences. The Birmingham dialect is significantly different from that of people in Yorkshire, and again from those in Newcastle (Jordies). And so on.

"Hey, you sound like you come from Cornwall', said a fellow fruit picker during the summer of 1963. Together with a few friends who were also waiting to go to University, I was working on a local fruit farm, picking black currants, strawberries, raspberries, and anything else that needed harvesting by hand. Dormitories housed students from various parts of the U.K., and they worked alongside us in the fields. They were fascinated with our accent, and described us as 'speaking like Cornishmen'. Well, many seemed to have that view, though others chipped in with, "No. You speak like Americans". And indeed, there are similarities of accent with both those of Cornwall and of the USA. And our response?

"Well, you're from up north, and speak funny. This is proper English what we're speaking". Which was followed by hilarious laughter from those living in the dormitories.

In fact, it is said that there are 160 distinct dialects of English in the world, including many found in India, the United States, Australia, and other English speaking countries. But in England. there is the basic division of northern and southern dialects. Among the southern accents is Angle, with subdivisions of Norfolk and Suffolk.

Norfolk people have a very distinctive way of speaking, which is peculiar to the county. That, of course, is a sweeping generalisation. Neither Delia Smith nor Stephen Fry, nor indeed the King nor the Prince of Wales, who have residences in Norfolk, speak with Norfolk accents. And then there was Bernard Matthews with his bootiful turkey meat, and Allan Smethurst, the singing postman, asking, "Hev yew gart a loight, bor?" 'Norfolk' involves unique pronunciations of vowels, and also consistent grammatical forms that are rather different from standard English. And within Norfolk itself, the dialect cannot be said to be homogenous, and there are also blends and merges across the borders into the neighbouring counties.

The Norfolk accent is similar to that of Suffolk, but very different from that of Cambridgeshire and Lincolnshire, from which Norfolk is separated by the Fens. This region was once largely impassable, which contributed to a relative degree of isolation of Norfolk, and the distinctive accent in the county. Today, the dialect is less distinct than a century or more ago. One could say that it has become rather diluted, and for several reasons. Travel has become so much easier, and people move around significantly more than, say, a century ago. On leaving school, it was usual to find work, and a marriage partner, locally, and generations of the same family would reside within a relatively small area.

*******

"Take a look at my teeth, and let me know what you can do. I haven't always gone as regularly as I should, but now I have time, and quite frankly, expense is no problem. Just do the very best you can for me". He was a new patient, new to the practice, recently retired and having sold his property in the Home Counties, was awash with cash. You get a lot more property for your money in Norfolk! And a statement like that was not uncommon, especially in my county practice, where immigrants from the London area would find their dream cottage in a rural Norfolk village. However, with a significant number of retirees (and younger people commuting, or working from home), drifting into the county, the dialect was heard a little less often. It was becoming 'diluted'.

The radio, previously known as the wireless, was invented around 1895-1896 by the Italian Guglielmo Marconi. It was soon produced commercially, and became common in the late 1920s and early 1930s. By

1934, 60% of the nation's households possessed a wireless. This exposed the people of Norfolk, along with the rest of the UK, to a much purer form of spoken English. Most broadcasters at that time spoke with an 'Oxford accent'. The effect of this on the way the people of Norfolk spoke at the time was minimal, and yet over the course of many decades, the effect was cumulative, resulting in dilution of the accent, as mentioned above.

'Putting the cart before the horse,' sounds like a traditional rural Norfolk idiom. But no-one in the county spoke of putting the cart before the horse until American films arrived in the country, and even more so since the advent and popularity of television. Today, people in Norfolk 'get the show on the road', can be 'fired' from their employment, and if so, may well 'bite the bullet'. These expressions are all American English, and have influenced the way people throughout the U.K., including my home county, speak. Norfolk is changing!

In addition to the Norfolk dialect having been diluted by the advent of radio and television, which can be found in almost every home, by cinema, and especially American films, and by the drift of retirees from the Home Counties, there is another significant factor involving people like myself. It is said within the county, that Norfolk birds come home to roost. Before the 20th century, they rarely flew away, but that has changed. Greatly. Returning to roost in Norfolk can have quite an effect on the overall dialect.

We fly away for a while, deposit a little of our accent, and return to dilute the overall dialect. This has proved true for me, and for many of my friends. Joe Woodcock and I have known each other since September 1956, and we can both remember the occasion well. It was our first day at the Paston School, in form 1B, after passing our 11+ examination. Joe was born locally, and lived locally. As a young man, he met Rosie at a mutual friend's birthday party. Wow – for Joe it was love at first sight; for Rosie, it was the start of several months of considering... weighing it up... praying even... However, taking Rosie for a week in a Methodist hostel in Cornwall did the trick, and they were soon married. Joe trained and qualified as a chartered surveyor in the Valuation Office in Norwich, and was almost immediately promoted to a position in Chichester for 3 years, and then to Walton-on-Thames, with the promise/threat of further promotion to central London. 'Noooo,' thought Joe, in anguish of mind and torment of spirit. 'I am a Norfolk bor.' And forthwith, the family took a step of faith with drop in salary, and returned to start again in Norfolk, under that big blue sky. "One of the best decisions we ever made", he added. Joe and Rosie joined us for lunch recently, with another 1956 first-former from the Paston School - David Buck and his wife Sandra. Except David was a bright boy, had passed his 11+ *first time*, and had therefore been put into 1A. David had left the county and gone to live and work in Dorset, which is a beautiful part of the world - but, like Chichester, it just isn't Norfolk. They returned to the county. David and Sandra have lived for many years in Little Melton, a charming village just south-west of Norwich. And then I consider my own journey in life. Born, brought up and educated in Norfolk, I trained in London, went into practice in Shaftesbury, an enchanting Saxon hilltop town in the very north of Dorset. But as I have just stated - it just isn't Norfolk, and for the past 50 years, I have lived back in the county of my birth. Norfolk birds come home to roost.

In my case, this certainly had an effect on the way I speak. Having worked on the land at the age of 18, where for 3 months I was surrounded by farm labourers speaking the Norfolk dialect with some of the heaviest accents in the county, I did not want to stand out as being too different. I tried to speak like they spoke. And by the time I reached London, to study at University, I was asked, "Where on earth do *you* come from?" My reply, that "Oi come frarm Narfick" simply brought polite smiles from the well-mannered, and howls of mirth from others. To cut a fairly long story short, I thought hard, identified the most important aspects of the Norfolk dialect, and did something about it. It might be said that my Norfolk accent was significantly diluted. And when I returned to roost, so to speak, I contributed to the dialect being spoken just that little bit less in the county.

Yet having said that new phrases, not least from across the Atlantic, have taken hold in Norfolk speech, and in the UK generally, it is also true that at least one word, previously exclusive to our Norfolk vocabulary, is now being used *outside* the county. In an earlier book, I referred to the Norfolk words 'bishy barnabee', which mean 'ladybird'. It was added to the Oxford English Dictionary in 2018.

*******

"Mingin's garn and bitten me", said Stalky. "Oi reck'n it was when we wuz after the parllywiggles".

In fact, a number of us had been bitten by mingins, which was a risk one took when trying to collect pollywiggles. One would become so focused on looking for the pollywiggles, and when spotted, diving in with the net and scooping them out, that a mingin on the back of the neck could pass unnoticed. Or even on the forearm.

Stalky was rubbing his arm, and sure enough, there was quite a bite. His mum had put some TCP antiseptic on it, but it itched, as mingin bites do. And then I found that I had a few mingin bites. I could feel the itch on the back of my neck, but the ones on my arms and legs were quite red and fiery.

"One wuz buzzin' in moi lug", said Gully. "Oi dinged it, and squarshed it. 'E woon't be boitin' noo one noo more".

I have read that accents are difficult, if not impossible, to put onto paper. An accent involves the emphasis of various words, syllables and vowels by stress or pitch. One tries to convey something of the pronunciation, but the stress and pitch are, for me, beyond the written word. However, the sentence above translates as follows:

"One was buzzing in my lug", said Gully. "I dinged it and squashed it. He won't be biting no-one no more". Or one could write, " One was buzzing in my ear. I hit it and squashed it. He won't be biting anyone anymore".

And the mingin? Mosquitos are commonly referred to as mingins by Norfolk people, especially those in rural areas where the dialect is a little more protected from the dilution alluded to earlier.

*******

"Oi driv to Narrich, said 'Keep yew a-trorshin' to my mairts, but blust, arn the way back, it snew. Thass a rummun, I thought".

If you read that aloud, you will find yourself 'speaking Norfolk'. But let me firstly rewrite it in Norfolk English, a partial translation, so to speak.

"I drove to Norwich, said 'Keep you a troshing' to my mates, but blast, on the way back, it snowed. That's a rum one, I thought".

Troshing? Rummun, or rum one?

Norfolk has, for decades, had words, pronunciations and grammar, that have been something of a mystery to those from outside the county. Oi. Driv. Yew. Troshing. Snew. It is highly unlikely that you would come across either the words or the pronunciation anywhere else in the U.K. Or the world. But let's have one further look at the above sentence.

Just supposing you were a BBC news reader (around fifty years ago, when they spoke Oxford English, rather like the King), then you would have said -

"I drove to Norwich, said 'Goodbye' to my friends; but blast, on the way home it snowed. That's unexpected, I thought".

The grammar can be quite different from Oxford English, introducing words that you would not hear elsewhere.

Driv instead of drove, shew instead of showed, and snew instead of snowed.

*******

I have mentioned, in the companion volume (*Big Blue Sky*, 2022), how our dialect can cause a degree of mirth amongst the better spoken, or somewhat confused folk from outside the county. A favourite amongst some of the younger members of the family, and the cause of many a snigger, especially with those who resided outside Norfolk, is that churchgoers can sit in a poo on Sunday mornings, whilst regular worshippers tend to sit in their own poo, if you follow me. Likewise, drivers stop at fool stations, where, if busy, there might be a coo. There are other examples.

"My dad's having trouble with his bowels", said my schoolmate Lenny. "It's really getting him down".
"Tell him to eat more fruit", I volunteered. But Lenny just stared at me, and said, "I can't see how fruit can help him. The whole team's got a problem".

With regard to the conversation with Lenny, I had a distinct advantage, in that my paternal grandfather lived in Peterborough. And played bowls. He would talk about it. *Bowls.* But had he lived in Norfolk all his life, and especially if he had had little contact with 'them foreigners' from outside the county, he might well have said he played *bowels.*

As I have said already, our Norfolk dialect has become diluted over the years, and today, a greater number of Norfolk people play bowls, whilst a proportionately lesser number play bowels.

"Off to play bowels tonight", says my friend Mike. "Love my bowels, I do".
"Mike, you need *guts* to play bowels", I jest in response. But it goes over his head, and he stares back, thinking '*guts* to play bowels? Barrie does say some strange things at times'.

*******

My mates and I would love to build dens, both around the disused stables in our garden, and even more so in the woods behind our home. Those in the woods would be constructed of fallen branches from a variety of trees, and propped together, resembling a cross between a North American tepee, and a bird's nest. The vegetation camouflaged the den to some extent, but we were living in an imaginary world. We were hunters, or fugitives, or jungle-dwellers. Anyone walking through the woods would hear quite loud voices reduced to a whisper, and walk past pretending not to notice the structure. Unless they had a dog. And then again, if Roger the Rough found your den, and decided that you were not friends at that time, he would probably pull it down. And in that case, a heated exchange of words might well take place.

"Yer fumble-fisted idiot, Rarger. Yew shouldn't ortera dunnit, cos Oi'm gonna tell on yew", said Gully. "And look at yer - yer awl of a muckwash, bor. Yew stink".

"He stunk frarm the toime he gart up this morning", said Stalky.

"Hold yew hard, or Oi'll bash yer", said Roger the Rough. And then he turned round, and went lolloping off.

In the account of the incident above, there are some obvious instances of the Norfolk accent in the pronunciation. So Roger becomes Rarger, I becomes Oi, and got becomes gart.

However, there are also examples of the Norfolk dialect apart from pronunciation. 'You should not have done that' becomes 'Yer shouldn't ortera dunnit'. That is an

"Let's build a den", said Gully….. branches were added….

expression quite commonly used in Norfolk conversations. 'Stank' becomes 'stunk', and in the same way, sang would become sung. 'The song he sang' becomes 'The song he sung'.

There are also a few words and expressions not found outside the county, except when Norfolk people are on holiday.

Fumble-fisted means clumsy.
Awl of a muckwash means sweating.
Bor can be translated boy, and yet is used a little more widely, and not exclusively when addressing a boy. Or indeed, a male.
Hold yew hard means stop.
Lolloping means strolling, and yet usually conjures up a picture of an energetic walk, and maybe a slow motion gallop.

*******

"Let's build a den", said Gully. It sounded like a great idea, and we spread out through the wood, and each returned with branches of differing lengths, and from a variety of trees. The low branch of a nearby tree was just asking to be used as a horizontal beam, and the gathered branches were pitched against it from both sides. Other branches were added, and being some yards from the nearest trail that walkers used, stood a good chance of remaining unnoticed, if we kept quiet when people approached. Perhaps we needed a lookout on sentry duty, and Shadley, being shorter than the rest of us, was stationed in a bush with a clear view of the trail, and close enough to us to make a "*Shhh*" that could be heard by us, and hopefully not by the approaching walker. But the silence was broken, as Gully suddenly shouted,

"PISHAMIRES. 'Undreds of 'em. They've gart up moi trarsers".

Gully jumped up, demolishing part of the pitched wall, while from the bush came, "*Shhh* yew lart. People will hair yew".

Too late. Nobody wanted pishamires up their trousers, and the rest of us were springing up, scratching, and trying to put distance between ourselves and the den. And of course, the pishamires.

Gully had his trousers down to his ankles, and was scratching furiously, and Stalky and I were banging our trousers legs with our hands, in order to squash any of the offending creatures, before standing on one leg and shaking the other energetically, in the hope that pishamires might drop out.

As it happened, Gully said he had received 3 or 4 bites, and no doubt it was the first one that had alerted him. Stalky claimed 2 bites, and I simply found a few pishamires running over the outside of my trousers and shirt. And Shadley? He virtually fell out of his bush, and rolled around on the ground, howling with uncontrollable laughter, and shouting, 'Wot a larf'.

It seemed from the number of pishamires running around, that we had built our den over a nest. We would be more careful in future, and check out the site to make sure we would be safe from such a ground attack.

My mother was highly amused. "Gully had pishamires in his trousers, biting his legs?", she said. "You mean that he had ants in his pants!"

Shadley virtually fell out of his bush, howling with uncontrollable laughter, and shouting, "Wot a larf".

\*\*\*\*\*\*\*

It was another day, and another adventure. We had checked for pishamires, and decided we were quite safe.

No pishamires. But there was going to be a different surprise, although of a more harmless nature, and involving creatures with peculiarly Norfolk names. In other parts of Britain, they had other names.

Moving to Wroxham, and finding that our new home had disused stables and other outbuildings in the garden, was indeed exciting for an eight year old boy. And then to find loose panels in the fencing behind the back garden, and access into some sizeable woods, was the icing on the cake. This property was clearly full of potential for amazing adventures, and in many ways those dreams were realised.

The stables and other outbuildings may not have been in a pristine state of repair, but nor were they about to collapse. There were weathered concrete blocks, bricks which had seen better days, and planks of wood of varying lengths and widths. Had they never been used? Were they evidence that other buildings had indeed collapsed? But a young lad of my age did not ask or think such questions. Such debris was there to be used.

My mother was a creative lady, and thought we could use one stable as a theatre. Concrete blocks and bricks and sections of tree trunk were gathered from the garden. We scavenged planks of wood that had seen far better days, and removed protruding nails and caked-on mud. These, placed on small stacks of concrete blocks and bricks, or a tree stump, made rickety seating for the audience. Rugs hung from the rusty railings, that looked at home in the stable, though I could not imagine their function. The rugs were curtains, behind which was the stage.

Shadley and Gully came round to inspect the premises. Well, they were going to be ushers and curtain pullers and so needed a degree of familiarity.

"That front bench is on tha huh", said Gully.
Shadley took a look at it. "Ain't really. It's the loight what does it. It's not really on tha huh, Gully".
"Well Oi think it is, and they'll all fall orf", said Gully. No doubt we would find out later.

Mother thought of a simple story, and wrote the script. Fred was a convict who we found hiding in one of our sheds, and he wanted to go straight. So we found him a job in the pub at the top of the road. And we all lived happily ever after. That was the story.

Needless to say, mother gave my sister Julia and myself star parts. Roger the Rough was well type-cast as Fred, and Shadley and Gully showed people to their seats, even if some were 'on tha huh'. The audience? The parents, maybe 15 in total, of our friends who lived in the same road as us, largely because their children were involved in the production. Mother was the prompter, and found herself quite busy. The whole play lasted around 20 minutes, and was followed by tea and biscuits.

As the mums and dads started drifting away, Roger, Gully, Shadley and Stalky stayed behind to dismantle the theatre.

"Look! Barneypigs", said Stalky. "You've got barneypigs living in your stable".

And sure enough, there were two barneypigs trotting along the concrete floor.

"Let's race 'em" said Shadley. "Get one of those planks and put it *really* on tha huh, and we'll race 'em down it". But the barneypigs had other ideas, and as soon as Shadley tried to pick his up, it rolled into a little grey ball.

"We can still race 'em", said Stalky. And for the following 5 or 10 minutes, rolled them down the plank that had been placed 'on tha huh'. And then the novelty was over, and the 2 barneypigs were left as 2 grey balls at the foot of the plank. It did not take very long to tidy up the stable, and by that time, the barneypigs had unrolled, and scuttled away.

Barneypigs are curious little creatures, feeding on rotting vegetation, fungi, and sometimes, their own faeces. They don't pee, but eliminate waste products, such as ammonia, by passing it out through their shells as a gas. The resulting odour is responsible for the 'pig'. In other parts of the country they are variously known as chisel-hogs, chuggy-pigs, sow-pigs, gramer-pigs, and granny-sows. In fact, *Country Life* magazine found 176 different nicknames for the creatures. Another study found that 94% of all nicknames involve the word pig. As a young lad, I thought they resembled miniature armadillos, but most books on nature refer to them as wood lice.

'On the huh' means that the object referred to is not on the level. This expression is used quite commonly and widely within the county.

And now for a little irregular Norfolk grammar. 'It' becomes 'that', so when others might say, "It smells funny, and it is a nice day", the sentence in Norfolk dialect would be, "That smell funny, and thass a nice day". And yet 'who', 'which' and 'that' are all replaced with 'what'. So, 'That present what you give me". And note, the past tense has been changed to the present.

Most of my childhood stories are from over 60 years ago. Time passes, and most things change. I suspect that 60 years before Gully, Shadley, Stalky, Sludge, myself and others were concerned with pollywiggles, pishamires, mingins and barney pigs, there was an even greater number of our age with similar vocabularies. And likewise, I suspect that there are less today, because as I have written earlier, the dialect, like most others, is becoming diluted.

The dialect has always been more pronounced in the countryside than in urban areas. And similar to other regions, it is more common amongst those working on the land, or jobbing labourers, than amongst the traditional professions and managerial classes. The accent is sometimes described as broad Norfolk. The stronger the accent, the 'broader' it is described as. 'A really broad accent'. Also, Norfolk people are called Norfolk Dumplings, because flour dumplings used to be a significant part of the diet. I shall return to the subject of dumplings.

FOND is the acronym for *Friends of the Norfolk Dialect*, founded in 1999, with aims of recognition and preservation of the Norfolk dialect, and for 'Norfolk' to be taught in the county's schools. Maybe not all of their aims will be realised, but they are helping keep the Norfolk dialect alive.

So let me close this chapter with some items from the Norfolk dialect which are still widely used today.

Thas a rummun = that's strange
Wha' a load of ole squit = what a load of nonsense
Are yer awlrite bor? = Hello! How are you?
Bred and born = born and bred
Come on t' rain = started to rain
At the finish = in the end (I passed my exam at the finish)
Good on yer = good for you. Also used in New England, where many East Anglian emigrants settled.
He dint ortera dunnit = he should not have done it
Abed = in bed
Afront = in front
Agin = against, or next to
Ahind = behind
Cushies = sweets
Forrads = forwards
Gawp = stare
Hint = have not
Hinttut = isn't it
Hull = hurl
Mardle = chat
Mob = tell off
Shiver = splinter
Suffun = something
Tuffee = toffee

All of which, and more, can be described as *Normal for Norfolk!*

# Chapter Three

## Norfolk Fayre

*Norfolk dumplings, Cromer crabs, samphire, kippers,*
*bloaters, and breakfast curry.*

"Thruppence worth of chips, please", said the little curly-haired boy, head and shoulders just about clearing the counter top.

The portly gentleman, clad in greased-smeared protective apron, looked non-plussed for a moment. Then he gave a big grin and said, "And thruppence worth of chips you shall have". A wire mesh scoop deposited a generous pile of chips onto a sheet of grease proof paper, to which was added an outer covering of two pages of the *Daily Mirror*. "Enjoy them, sonny", he smiled, as I slipped back to my father's car. It was Friday evening.

That was my first experience of a fish and chip shop, and back home, the chips were shared out with the family. We had been visiting relatives, and this was an evening treat. We were almost home when my father had drawn into the curb, pointed to the chippy and said, "Go and ask for thruppence worth of chips". He gave me a thruppenny bit, and I climbed out of the car and followed instructions.

There was more than a handful of chips each. This little treat proved popular, and was repeated the following Friday, and again a week later. Thruppence worth of chips. We were at home the Friday after that, when father caught my eye, grinned, and said, "Anyone fancy chips?"

There was a chorus of "Yes please", as he added, "It's a short walk. Let's go together". Ten minutes later, father and son stood at the counter. "Thruppence worth of chips, please", said my father. The response took us both by surprise, as Mr. Tubby looked my father in the eye and replied, "We don't do thruppence worth of chips. We start at fourpence".

"But my son has had thruppence worth of chips from you the past three or four Fridays", said my father, looking somewhat bemused.

"He certainly has", said the vendor of chips. "But no-one else has, because we stopped selling thruppence worth of chips over a year ago. But I couldn't disappoint the little lad".

My father pulled a penny out of his pocket, laid it beside his thruppenny bit, saying, "Sorry - it's a while since I bought chips. And thank you for accommodating to young Barrie here".

That was in 1954, when pennies, ha'pennies and thruppenny bits were in everyday use. It was 'old money', where the thruppenny bit was a twelve-sided coin of nickel brass, worth three old pennies, or one eightieth of a pound, or one quarter of a shilling. It had superseded the previous round thruppenny bit, made of silver. With decimilisation in 1971, all old coins were withdrawn. But fish and chips continued to be one of the favourite, best-selling fast foods in the U.K., and especially in Norfolk, with its 100 miles or so of coastline.

However, fish and chips did not originate in Norfolk. Lancashire and London both lay claim to birthing this incredibly popular dish, and both played a significant rôle. The potato was introduced to England in the 16th century, and it was during the 17th century that western Sephardic Jews settled in England, bringing with them their culinary skills of frying fish in a similar manner to the chippies of today. The French and the Belgians both claim to have first fried potatoes as chips, or *frites*. Certainly, there was a recipe for chips published in England in 1817. The first purpose-designed fishing boats were constructed by David Allan in Leith in 1875. Shortly after, the introduction of trawlers in the North Sea dramatically increased the number of cod and haddock caught, which were distributed widely and speedily with the advent and spread of the railway network in the late 19th century.

Chips were a cheap, staple food in the industrial north of England in the mid-19th century, whilst fried fish became popular in the east end of London at the same time. It was around 1860 that Joseph Malin, an Ashkenazi Jewish immigrant opened the first fish and chip shop in Bow, east London. It thrived, and continued in business for over a century. And around the same time, or just a few years later, John Lees opened a similar establishment in Mossley, near Oldham, and that too rapidly became extremely busy. By 1910, there were over 25,000 fish and chips shops across the U.K., and by 1930, there were over 36,000. However, the number had declined to around 10,000 by 2009.

Charles Dickens mentions chips in *A Tale of Two Cities*, and Alfred Hitchcock was brought up in a flat over a fish and chip shop in London. In 1928, Harry Ramsden opened his first fish and chip shop in Guiseley, West Yorkshire. In a single day in 1952, the shop served 10,000 portions of fish and chips, and gained an entry in the Guinness Book of Records. During both the first and second world wars, fish and chips was one of the few food items exempted from rationing.

Fish and chips was increasingly associated with seaside resorts, and the expansion of the railways in the late 19th century, brought huge numbers of holiday makers to the coastal towns of Norfolk. Sleepy fishing villages became thriving holiday resorts. Hunstanton, Cromer, and Great Yarmouth especially flourished, and hosted a plethora of fish and chip shops. A number of my childhood years were spent in Wroxham (several fish and chip shops), though my parents regarded Great Yarmouth (innumerable fish and chip shops) as the nearest thing to heaven on earth. I lived in Norfolk, and from that first visit to a chippy in 1954, I loved chips. And soon after, fried fish, and particularly, cod.

"Anything fresher is still swimming out there", said the ruddy-faced Cromer fisherman, as he delivered his catch to the local seafood restaurant. Today, Norfolk fish and chip shops, and restaurants, win national awards. Local fishermen, using small boats like their fathers, and their fathers before them, bring their catch ashore at first light, and it is just a matter of hours before they are fried and sitting on a plate in front of the customer. *Mary Jane's, Rocky Bottoms, No.1 restaurant* and a host of other seafood eateries, thrive along the Norfolk coast. Wendy and I love them. Love Norfolk. Love fish and chips.

"Yuck! Predigested peas", I groaned. Obviously, it's all a matter of taste, but garden peas are the real thing, whereas mushy peas are simply..... mushy. Predigested, perhaps? Maybe they are of medieval origin, and I am sure it is true that they are rich in protein, and they have been popular since the 1970s - but No!

"Curry sauce on your chips, sir?" No way! I maybe addicted to curry, but not with my fish and chips. That, to my mind, is a northern affliction, and I will stay free of it, thank you. "Ketchup, sir?" No thank you. Apparently ketchup originated in Vietnam, where it was produced from fermented fish, even though the blame is usually, wrongly, laid at the door of the Americans. (And, of course, it's made from tomatoes today). I don't care - I don't want it. Maybe some tartar sauce, but ketchup? No thank you.

*******

A red army from Russia was advancing on the U.K. and there were rumours of sightings on the beaches of Yorkshire. How long before they reached Norfolk?

Cromer crabs are renowned for their taste, and there are few Norfolk restaurants that do not include Cromer Crab Salad on their menu during the summer months. Slimming? Low calorie? The last time I was served such a salad, it was accompanied by around 15 new potatoes! The earliest record of Cromer Crabs is found in *A Guide about Cromer*, which was published in 1800 by Edmond Burtell, where one reads 'Lobster, crabs, whiting and cod-fish and herring are all caught in the finest perfection'. The crabs have been a staple in the region for centuries.

The inhabitants of Cromer will tell you in no uncertain terms, that the Cromer crab is no ordinary crab. Connoisseurs of shellfish, and gourmets with discerning palates, will immediately identify this submarine celebrity by its sweet, unique flavour, and tender texture. The waters off the shores of Sheringham and Cromer are relatively shallow, and the crabs live on the chalk reef, filtering in the clean, unmuddied waters.

There are many different species of crab living around the shores of the U.K. The smallest and rarest is a tiny hermit crab, which is only 6mm in length. It does not have a common name, and so is known as *Clibanarius erythropus*, which is Latin for 'soldier, clad in mail, with red legs'. None were found between 1985 and March 2016. But it is very small. Other types include various swimming crabs, the spider crab, the shore crab or green crab (found inhabiting rock pools), and the velvet crab.

And then there was the red army from Russia - which wasn't. Giant red crabs were found on Yorkshire beaches in 2021, and were initially thought to be an invasive species from Russia, growing to over 6 feet in length, and devouring crustaceans smaller than themselves. Like Cromer crabs. The scare was over when the Natural History Museum identified them as Norwegian king crabs, or stone crabs.

But the Cromer crab is the brown crab, or edible crab. It is said that it has a relatively high proportion of white to brown meat compared with brown crabs caught elsewhere, again enhancing its flavour, and ensuring its appearance on the menus of high-end restaurants from Lands End to John O'Groats. And especially in Norfolk. There are understandably many recipes, including *Crab Thermidor*, but with the above mentioned salad, a little lemon juice and a pinch of black pepper, you're in for a treat.

They are caught live in pots, a tradition going back centuries. Small ones are thrown back into the sea, and live to fight, and breed, another day. This is a sustainable method of harvesting, and ensures that every crab reaching a dinner plate has had at least one breeding season. This industry provides both work and income for the towns of Sheringham and Cromer, on the North Norfolk coast, and is celebrated with the annual Crab and Lobster Festival, starting with a Friday night concert in the theatre on Cromer pier, and continuing through the weekend.

The World Crabbing Competition may not have been heard of by many outside Norfolk (or in Norfolk), but takes place annually on a Sunday in August. Cromer pier is the location, where both teams and individuals can register, and compete to catch the greatest number of crabs, or the largest crab.

"Nurse, will you go and fetch my next patient from the waiting room please", was a recurring request during my days in dental practice. But on one occasion, I added a little more. "And be careful not to laugh, because she always walks sideways". Karen grabbed the patient's notes and set off at pace towards the waiting room. Suddenly there was a peal of laughter, and she returned to the surgery, waving the notes at me. She had looked to see the patient's name, and it was Mrs. Crabbe. From Cromer, of course.

*******

While we are in the North Norfolk area, and speaking about crabs, I must also mention one or two other coastal villages renowned for their fayre, and say a few words about their respective shellfish. Norfolk is famous for Brancaster mussels and Stiffkey cockles. But let's just give the lobster a mention, as it has similarities to a crab, and they can be found together on the chalk beds off the

North Norfolk coast, as well as on dinner plates in the county's restaurants.

Like Cromer crabs, the lobsters are especially succulent, sweet and tasty. The chalk reef off the North Norfolk coast is said to be the longest in the world. I have read that this chalk ridge includes the white cliffs of Dover, the white horse hill carvings in Wiltshire, and the highest point in East Anglia, the Cromer Ridge. The water is relatively warm, and both crabs and lobsters have a wealth of food to scavenge. The native lobster is blue. If it lives in deep water, it is deep blue. If it lives in shallow water, it is light blue.

Lobster pots are constructed of a wooden framework, with netting forming a tunnel, leading to the chamber (sometimes called the kitchen), where bait of fish is placed. The lobster can find the way in, but cannot find or penetrate the tunnel to get out. The pot sits on the sea floor, marked by a buoy on the surface. A good catch can be several lobsters in the pot, and perhaps a few crabs too. They can be caught all the year round, are reckoned to be bigger when caught in the winter, though the weather is more conducive to fishing for them in the summer. And the tourist demand is from May to September.

And now an amazing fact about lobsters - they do not age like almost every other creature, and they never die of old age. Unlike me, they do not slow down, weaken or lose fertility as the years pass. An enzyme called telomerase 'mends' damaged DNA. So they usually die of disease - or end up on a dinner plate.

\*\*\*\*\*\*\*

In the 1800s, it was a brick kiln. Then it became an agricultural store. Then, in 2008, it fell down! Richard Matthews, a local fisherman, and Alison, his wife, a cook, saw the potential. They rebuilt the ruins into a fabulous seafood restaurant. *Rocky Bottoms*, in West Runton, opened in 2015, and thrives. There are truly amazing dishes, piled up with seafood. Likewise, along the coast at Salthouse, is the quirky *Cookies Crab Shop*. It has been described as a flinty shack, or less flatteringly, as a glorified shed. Just occasionally, it is flooded with seawater. You take your own beer or wine, and it is probably best to go to the toilet before arriving, though there's always the pub across the road. But for three generations, incredible plates of lobster, crab, shellfish, whitefish, smoked fish, and more, have been served to seafood *aficionados*. It was a well-kept secret, though Stephen Fry discovered it long ago. Today, on a sunny, summer day, it can be heaving. It is a Norfolk institution.

Did you know that mussels have muscles? And did you know you can tell the sex of a mussel from its colour? And who would guess that they are sown as seeds, and grow to maturity over 2 years? A mussel has a right and left shell, hinged, and held together by adductor muscles. When cooked, the muscle usually becomes detached, and the shell opens. Orange mussels are female, and creamy white ones are male. And the best place to find them in the U.K. is Brancaster. Why? Once again, it's the offshore chalk reef.

Brancaster mussels are grown on beds, and harvested from October through to March, as opposed to the industrially produced mussels on ropes that are harvested throughout the year. And which, would you guess, are the succulent, plump, fleshy ones? Grown on beds where land meets sea, they drink at high tide and rest at low. This gives them character, distinctive flavour, and a longer shelf life. And they are not harvested mechanically as the industrialised ones are, but by traditional raking, as in the 20th century. And as in the 19th century. And long before that.

Until the latter part of the 20th century, van loads of Brancaster mussels would be transported to the Midlands daily. There, in some of our large industrialised cities, they would find their way to market stalls, where the working man would pick up a bag, and take home for his dinner. But restaurants started leaning more towards locally produced, home-grown fayre for their menus, and today, 'Brancaster blues', as they are known locally, can be found in some of our more sophisticated restaurants - *and* on the Nottingham market stalls.

*Moules marinière* is a popular presentation of mussels. Across the Channel, it would be served with *"Bon appetite!"*, whereas in cafés and pubs along the Norfolk coast, your more than ample portion will probably be served with, "There yew goo. Injoy!" Or in some of our more exclusive seafood restaurants, *"Bon appetite"*. But maybe you would like to cook your own? If so, there are any number of vendors along the North Norfolk coast, in the towns and villages of Thornham, Blakeney, Wells, Cley and others on, or a mile or two from, the A149.

Stiffkey is an enchanting North Norfolk village, with traditional flint cottages lining the main street. Situated in an area of outstanding natural beauty on the river Stiffkey, it was recorded in the 11th century as having 54 households, which put it in the 20% of largest settlements in England. In the 15th century, a water mill gave the village its identity, until it fell into disrepair in the late

19th century. And today, the village is famous for cockles.

Like their Brancaster relatives, they are known locally as 'blues'. But whereas the blue of the mussels further along the coast is a natural colouring, the blue of the Stiffkey cockles is leached out of the mud from which they are harvested. And locally, the pronunciation of Stiffkey is Stewkey. Hence, Stewkey blues.

The cockles are found in colonies, just north of Stiffkey, on the seaward side of salt marshes where they live about an inch under the surface, in a mixture of mud and sand. They have traditionally been raked from the mud, and washed in seawater. They are usually boiled, sold from stalls, and eaten with pepper and vinegar. Stewkey blues are said to have a rich, refreshing, slightly salty, shellfish flavour.

Sea beans (USA), sea asparagus (British Columbia, Canada), and crow foot greens (Nova Scotia) are all names for samphire. It is seaweed! However, some call it a marine vegetable, and in Norfolk it is called 'samfur'. Well, that is how it is pronounced.

It grows on coastal mudflats and salt marshes, and North Norfolk has the largest area of salt marshes in the country. And so it is not surprising that the county also produces more samphire than any other part of the U.K. It is harvested during the summer months of June through to September, and is eaten as a vegetable with seafood, or perhaps as a starter, lightly boiled, and with butter, pepper and vinegar.

The word is actually a corruption of *Saint Pierre*. Saint Peter is the patron saint of fishermen, and samphire was sometimes taken on voyages, as like limes, its consumption helped prevent scurvy.

Although London restaurants import their samphire from Israel and Mexico, boiling it for a matter of seconds and serving in small portions, locals would laugh at this and strongly recommend eating it the Norfolk way. Boil it for around 15 minutes, pile your plate high, smother in molten butter, and add pepper. "Yew carnt beat our Narfick samfur, eaten tha Narfick way!"

*******

Two further Norfolk seafood items have to be given a mention – kippers and bloaters. Both are closely associated with Great Yarmouth, though kippers are produced in many other parts of the British Isles these days. Kippers are whole herrings which have been split, butterfly style, along their dorsal ridge, gutted, salted, and cold smoked over wood chips. They are a breakfast food – and I love them.

Bloaters are more exclusively associated with Great Yarmouth, and are also whole herrings. However, they are not gutted, and the head and tails are left *in situ*. Leaving the guts in produces a stronger flavour, sometimes described as 'gamey'.

"You have an unusual accent", said Douglas Farmer, senior registrar in dental conservation (fillings) at the London Hospital, where I was training to become a dentist back in the 1960s. "Where are you from?" I said that I came from Norfolk.

"Norfolk!" he bellowed. "Norfolk! Well, if you want to get on well here, and pass your exams, you'd better send me some bloaters. Love bloaters, I do, and can't seem to get them outside Norfolk". Douglas Farmer came from Devon.

*******

We are famous for our dumplings. Lancashire has its Eccles cakes, Yorkshire has its puddings, Derbyshire has its Bakewell tarts – but we have Norfolk dumplings. They might have been more common in days past, but there are plenty around today.

Two dumpling shaped, middle-aged ladies glared at me. "How did you do that?" asked the one with the orange hair and red face. It was Tuesday evening, and I was at *WeightWatchers*, and at the weigh-in was told I had lost 3 pounds that week.

"Must have been the Indian restaurant last Tuesday", I suggested.

"Indian restaurant?" said the dumpling with green hair and multiple chins. "That's not fair".

"Or it could have been the Chinese take-away on Wednesday evening", I volunteered, causing further remarks concerning injustice and disbelief.

"You can't lose weight eating Indian curries and Chinese take-aways", said dumpling number 1. "You're cheating, aren't you!"

"No way", I replied. "I'll tell you my secret. I have an Indian curry after Weight Watchers on Tuesday evening, and a Chinese take-away on Wednesday evening. But I don't eat at all on Mondays, or until I've been weighed

"You can't lose weight eating Indian curries and Chinese take-aways", said Dumpling number 1. "You're cheating, aren't you!" I was at WeightWatchers.

on Tuesdays. And I try to walk 10 miles a day. I want to lose weight, you see".

"So do I", said Dumpling number 2. "But I've got to eat my 6 chocolate bars a day, and I'm not going walking nowhere. Or stop eating. I think you're cheating doing it that way".

People from the county have traditionally been called Norfolk dumplings. In 1811, the *Dictionary of the Vulgar Tongue* by Captain Grose has an entry under 'Norfolk Dumplins': 'A nick name, or term of jocular reproach to a Norfolk man; dumplings being a favourite food in that county'.

So dumplings were our favourite food in Norfolk once! It has been said that dumplings originated in the county in the early 17th century, with a corruption of the German word *klumpen* (lump). A true Norfolk dumpling is a swimmer, and floats in a stew, whereas one that goes to the bottom is a sinker. These are not recognised as true Norfolk dumplings, and are rumoured to originate in Suffolk. Also, the true Norfolk dumpling never contains suet.

Early dumplings were probably balls of bread dough, taken from the batch used to make the loaves. Today, milk, eggs and flour are generally agreed to be the basic ingredients. They are typically eaten with mince and potatoes, though recipes vary. Originally, their purpose was to cheaply fill the stomach, where meat might be in short supply.

*******

"Not more asparagus, Mummy. Can't we have cabbage, or sprouts?" was a repeated complaint at meal times in our home. For most people, asparagus was special, and probably expensive. They usually had cabbage and sprouts on their plates, and their children might probably have said, "Not more cabbage and sprouts, Mummy. Can't we have asparagus?" But my parents loved asparagus, and whenever we moved house (my father was a bank clerk, and was moved every few years), they would plant an asparagus bed as a priority. As a child, I soon got tired of it, though today I love it.

'Norfolk Asparagus - Next Layby' is a notice seen quite frequently besides Norfolk roads today. *Norfolk* asparagus? Asparagus has been a popular food in England since Roman times, and English asparagus is today reckoned to be the best in the world, due to its relatively slow growth in our climate, which makes it flavourful and tender. It is grown in many areas of England, and its season traditionally started on St. George's day (23rd April) through to the summer solstice (21st June). However, with climate change, these dates are tending to move forward to some extent. It is a desert plant, and thrives on sandy soil. Some Norfolk farms have acres and acres of asparagus spears, which are usually cut by hand. A recent problem for the 'industry' has been a shortage of workers to harvest the crop. And after the edible spears have been harvested, asparagus ferns grow, and are attractively used in flower arranging. That is something I remember well from my childhood days, and our domestic crop.

*'Norfolk Asparagus'* is a starter in restaurants. It is lightly steamed, and coated with Hollandaise sauce, and is a great way to celebrate St. George's day. But other

options are endless - simply as a vegetable, wrapped in prosciutto or bacon, as soup, in a tart, etc.

Small native woodland strawberries have been grown in Britain for centuries, and from the Middle Ages cultivated in domestic gardens. In the 16th century, the Virginia strawberry was brought over from America. It was sweeter, but quite small. The most significant change in strawberry production was the result of a French spy called, *Frézier*, being sent to Chile in the early 18th century. He was to report back on munitions and fortifications there, but happened to notice large strawberries growing on plants, and brought some back. They were almost tasteless, but were crossed with the woodland strawberry, and the rest is history.

Norfolk is a huge producer of strawberries. Earlier this year (2023), a local farm announced plans to increase its strawberry production to 750 tonnes a year. But around 65 years ago, a curly-haired lad would cycle from his home in North Walsham, during the long summer school holidays, and at various fruit farms at different times, spend the day picking (and consuming) ripe strawberries, before returning home with a pound or two (inflation would change that amount) in his pocket, and bright pink hands. As mentioned earlier, I worked on one farm for around 3 months, after leaving school in 1963, and they employed so many students during the summer months, that dormitories were constructed to house them. More recently, Eastern Europeans have provided much of the labour necessary, as strawberries continue to be handpicked.

I have yet to meet anyone who confesses to not liking strawberries. I was brought up in the days when you ate what you were given, and if you did not, you were liable to go hungry. That would seem to have changed today, though most of our grandchildren enjoy most foods. However, even during my childhood, there were pet hates quite commonly expressed when school dinners were served. School dinners were lunches served in the middle of the day - the terminology betrays the *clientele*. In fact, children like me attending state schools. Pet hates? - "Urggghhhh, it's stinking swede on my plate" or terrible turnip (the worst), or even pesky parsnips. But there was a choice of eating it or going hungry, and most chose not to go hungry. In those days, rural, agricultural Norfolk was very much a county of meat and 2 veg. However, that has changed dramatically over the years.

Are there particular dishes or drinks, where you can remember your 'first'? This Norfolk boy has several such memories, and probably because I was brought up in a family where meat, potatoes, and 2 veg was very much the order of the day, every day, and to consider anything even mildly spicy, could be described as wildly experimental and daring.

"Nana and Grandpa are taking us all out for high tea in a restaurant in Scole", said my mother. I was aged around 9 at the time, and enquired what 'high tea' was. Mother informed me that it was a little more than bread and butter and cakes, but not so much as 'dinner'. We arrived at the restaurant, and were shown to a table, where we took our seats. The menu seemed something of a mystery to me, but my mother suggested I try baked beans on toast. I had never heard of the dish before, and to this day can remember being overwhelmed by the most mouth-watering, flavoursome, delicious food I had ever come across. This was not the Norfolk I was used to. It would prove to be a rare treat, and I have never forgotten high tea in Scole that day.

"Here is a shilling, to go and buy a drink with. We have not been to a Butlin's Holiday Camp before, and we want you to really enjoy your time here", said my father, placing the silver coin in my hand and directing me towards a service hatch in the restaurant that seemed to accommodate hundreds of us. I had never heard of *Pepsi-Cola*, but I bought a can, and it proved to be another 'baked beans moment' - there were no words to adequately describe the experience, though 'exquisite' and 'delectable' might come close. Another 'first' encounter that this Norfolk boy remembers so well to this day.

But in the 1960s and 1970s, Norfolk people started becoming aware of a wider culinary experience, that the rest of the UK, and especially the larger multicultural cities, had enjoyed for a few decades. Since Roman times, spices had been brought from China and India along the ancient Silk Road through the Middle East and into Europe, and were prized amongst the wealthy. European explorers first reached India in 1498, and trade routes started to develop. London's first Indian restaurant, the *Hindustani Coffee House* opened in 1809, but it was in the latter part of the 20th century, with a significant influx of Asian immigrants, including chefs, to Europe, that the consumption of Asian food really started to expand.

Auntie Marie was a spinster, and it was said within the family, that she 'got around' – restaurants, golf clubs, cruises, and so on. We were staying with her in the home she shared with my paternal grandparents in Peterborough. It was around the year 1960, and she said, "There's a Chinese restaurant opened in the city. I can't think what they eat there, but let's go and see!" And what an evening it turned out to be, and even now, over 60 years later, I can recall the taste of some of that amazing exotic fayre, served in the *Great Wall* restaurant, in the city centre. Not only did it taste like heaven, but I had never felt so full in all my life. My sister implored me to stop eating, saying she could tell that I was going to be violently sick later. But I finished everything on my heaped-up plate, and it all stayed down. And that was the start of a life-long journey and passion for this Norfolk lad. Later on, in September 1963, I left home, and took up residence in Bloomsbury, in London WC1. I used to tell people in Norfolk that I was now living in the heart of London's WC! Just a stone's throw from the hall of residence where I lived was the first Indian restaurant that I was to cast my eyes on. It had the word *Bengal* in its name, but I do not recall the rest. However, if I had thought that Chinese food was an introduction to heaven, my first visit to the Indian restaurant immediately pushed Chinese food into second place, and from that evening on, there was no looking back. Returning to my parents' home in Norfolk periodically, I found that an Indian restaurant had opened in our only Norfolk city, Norwich. I visited, and found it was moderately well patronised. However, when I moved back to Norwich in 1974, Indian restaurants were appearing faster than the daffodils coming up in spring. They were packed, and it seemed that everyone in Norfolk was consuming Indian food. Well, especially in the city, though in the more rural areas, meat, potatoes, and 2 veg remained the staple.

"Heck! I had a korma once, and my mouth stung for 3 days. It was agony. You won't get me near a curry again!" said friend Ivan recently, when discussing menus for a businessmen's dinner. Ivan is 'old Norfolk', the sort of Norfolk I grew up in, and typical of his generation in rural parts. But a *korma*, so mild and creamy, stung his

100

mouth? Maybe he was the victim of a practical joke, or perhaps he ordered by numbers and got it wrong. Today, there are restaurants and take-aways of every ethnicity known to man, not just in the city of Norwich, but seemingly in every town and many villages across the county.

"Grandpa, you have raised cooked breakfast to a whole new level!" said my grandson Elisha, after I told him of a planned culinary experience I had in mind when quite a number of family members were going to invade in the summer of 2021. The seeds were sown during a holiday in Indonesia some years earlier. I have a mission statement for my life, which is, 'I am on this earth to please God, and to make my wife's dreams come true'. One of Wendy's dreams was to see the orangutans in Borneo – so I took her there. It was our third morning at the hotel, and having consumed my daily bowl of breakfast cereal, I was making my way across the restaurant with a modest helping of bacon and eggs, when I saw a chef doling out what looked like curry and rice. Upon inspection, I was quite correct, and having dispatched the afore mentioned English cooked brekkie, I made my way to the curry chef, and received a portion of boiled rice and chicken curry. Now, what happened next might seem unbelievable to some, but on the way back to my table, I noticed another chef, who also appeared to be doling out curry and rice. I sauntered over to investigate, and sure enough, it was more curry. Fish curry. And so, having polished off my chicken curry, I had a small portion of fish curry. This was life as it was meant to be lived.

When visiting grandchildren in the various countries where they reside (Wendy and I have 6 daughters living in 5 different countries, along with our 20 grandchildren), there is usually the request at some point, "Grandpa, please cook us a curry while you are staying". I am always happy to oblige, but decided to push the boat out a little further during their visit in summer 2021, and so enquired of my 3 grandsons in France, "When you come to stay in August, would you like chicken curry and rice for breakfast one morning?" Elisha's response clinched the matter - I was raising cooked breakfast to a whole new level. Our 3 grandsons from France arrived, and 4 granddaughters from Amsterdam, and 2 grandsons and a granddaughter from our local city of Norwich. The New Zealand contingent were not joining us on that occasion, nor some of Wendy's, but there was an air of excitement, and unabated anticipation amongst those gathered. They watched and sniffed in awe one Wednesday evening, as I prepared Thursday's breakfast. And at around 9am the following morning, I served up 13 plates of boiled rice and medium chicken curry. 5 came back for seconds, and 3 came back for thirds. I was so proud of them all.

However, curry-flavoured breakfast did not originate in the kitchen of yours truly, but has been found in Norfolk, and indeed, the rest of the UK, for decades. It was my birthday, and Wendy decided I was to have a special treat, involving a short break away. For some time, I had been fascinated with the windmill at Cley on the North Norfolk coast, which had been converted into a hotel, and as we did not want to travel too far, this was the chosen venue.

There are a variety of rooms at the mill, and though a few staircases, a ladder and a trap-door seemed inviting, we felt that in view of Wendy having her arm in plaster, following a fall on a Dovedale walk, the ground floor was more appropriate. It was a beautiful room, irregular, quaint and cottagey, as was the rest of the mill. We later ascended a couple of flights of stairs, and enjoyed the view across the marshes, home to tens of thousands of sea birds, waders, geese, marsh harriers, etc. Dinner was excellent, and because it was my birthday, cheese and port were 'on the house'. A great place to stay, and a wonderful restaurant. But there was another surprise in store.

*Kedgeree*. Looking back, I am surprised that I had not come across kedgeree before. I am a Norfolk boy, but I have been around. I've walked on every continent and visited around 60 different countries, including India. However, kedgeree was new to me. There was a brief description of it on the menu, where I noticed the word 'curry'. That was it. "Kedgeree please!" And what a treat.

Kedgeree originates in India (surprise, surprise) and was consumed widely across the country for centuries. Some authorities say 'from the 14th century AD' and some 'from the 4th century BC'. So, for a long time! It was called *khichiri,* and was rice, spices, fried onions and lentils, though the recipe varied a little from place to place. When the colonialists arrived, the dish became very popular, and was a mainstay for breakfast in the days of the Raj. But the British introduced some changes, replacing dal with eggs, adding fish, and changing the name to kedgeree. Naturally, they brought the recipe back to the UK, where the Scottish take the credit for adding smoked fish at Findon, just south of Aberdeen. This was at the time when the stagecoach network was becoming popular, and ensured that the recipe was disseminated widely and quickly. Soon, kedgeree was popular nationwide, and especially in the breakfast rooms of country piles, where the gentry thought they had found heaven on earth. Today, it is virtually an all-day breakfast – and yet only discovered by yours truly, early in his eighth decade. What had I been missing.

Norfolk is a county with an extensive coastline, and a thriving fishing industry. No wonder that kedgeree is found on many hotel breakfast menus in the county. It was only a couple of months later that I discovered kedgeree again, on the menu at the Blakeney Hotel, another excellent establishment where Wendy and I stay most years. And yet, at *chez moi* in the village of Frettenham, it is chicken curry and rice that causes my grandchildren to beam with delight, and speak in such flattering terms of my culinary adventures. Shame on Wendy, who alone misses out, preferring to stay in bed and have toast and marmalade later. And congratulations to my amazing family, on their exceptional good taste. Cooked breakfast has been raised to a whole new level. In Norfolk. Curry – cooked by a Norfolk dumpling!

# Chapter Four

## Norfolk Transport

*Matt's tractor, Muddle and Go Nowhere, the Horse – and more*

The evening calm of light breeze, birdsong, and the fragrance of roses, was abruptly shattered by a loud clattering on our shingle drive. As a score of birds stopped singing, and took off in alarm, we lowered our glasses of chilled white wine, and swung round to view the intrusion.

"Are yer alroight?" said our good friend Matt, grinning broadly at our obvious consternation. "Oi was passing boi on moi tractor, and thought Oi'd drarp in on yer". He dismounted from his tractor, sauntered over to the patio, and drew up a chair.

Ruddy-faced Matt is a born and bred Norfolkman. He farms, he trims hedges, he supplies manure, and almost anything else of a rural nature that needs supplying, harvesting or fixing. And he often travels by tractor. He told us he had driven his tractor to Fakenham that morning, where there was an agricultural show, and though he was almost home now, thought he would drop in.

"You haven't driven that tractor all the way to Fakenham and back, have you?" I enquired, estimating that Fakenham must be around 30 miles away, that Matt's tractor was not exactly modern state-of-the-art, and that much of the road was single carriageway.

The evening calm of light breeze, birdsong, and the fragrance of roses, was abruptly shattered by a loud clattering on our shingle drive.

"Cors Oi hev", said Matt.
"And how many hundred cars and trucks were held up behind you?" I had to ask.
"Didn't look". Another big grin.

*Normal for Norfolk* would be an apt description of Matt's journey to Fakenham. Until a few years ago, the legal speed limit for tractors was 20 mph. Now it is 25 mph - but would Matt's tractor go that fast? One could only smile at the thought of hundreds of vehicles in a long snaking tailback, following Matt's ample frame perched behind the wheel of his tractor. No doubt a few horns gave a blast, and maybe there was some gesticulating and expletives, but this is Norfolk, where tractors are part of everyday life. Not that everyone in Norfolk travels by tractor, as some outside the county imagine. But there are certainly a huge number of tractors in Norfolk.

The tractor was derived from the traction engine, which itself was a development of the portable steam engine used on farms in the early 19th century. In 1859, the engine was mounted on wheels, and a large flywheel and thick leather belt used to drive the whole apparatus. It was now self-propelling - the traction engine had arrived. The first petrol-powered general purpose tractor was produced in Britain in 1901 by Dan Albone. Originally used for ploughing, they were soon widely employed for a multitude of agricultural tasks, including towing trailers, harvesting, fertilising, irrigation, and even calling in on friends for a refreshing glass of white wine during a pleasant summer evening.

Most countryfolk recognise the make of a tractor instantly, though city dwellers might not know the key. It is quite simple - blue is Ford, red is Massey Ferguson, orange is Renault, green is John Deere, and yellow is

JCB. There are many other makes and colours, but having walked the footpaths and bridleways of the county for many decades, those are my observations. Having said that, this has not always been the case, and until the 20th century, all tractors were black, grey or brown, regardless of make. Rather like motor cars.

Some Norfolk folk really love tractors. One local farmer boasted of 185 in his collection in 2015. On Boxing Day 2009, there was a procession of 170 tractors snaking their way from Larling to Great Hockham. They raised a lot of money for charity, but for anyone else travelling from Larling to Great Hockham, say by car, their lunch could well have been cold by the time they arrived.

Maybe Matt's tractor is a little slower than the motorists following him would wish for, but tractors do not have to be slow. The *JCB Fastrac* is the world's fastest production tractor, with a top speed of 43mph. But wait - an engineering team working for the company was not satisfied with that, and saw it as a challenge. After some modifications, Guy Martin, tractor driver *extraordinaire*, tore along a runway at Elvington Airfield in York, exceeding 153 mph at one point, and is now the Guinness Book of Records world tractor speed holder at 135.19 mph. But in Norfolk we are a little more relaxed and laid back, which is one reason some of us love the county and reside here.

*******

Snow had been falling all night, and there was no way we would be able to leave our cottage to even try and get to my dental practice. My wife and I walked along the top of the hedge on the right side of the lane, and our neighbours, Bob and Lynn, walked along the top of the hedge on the left side of the lane. We threw snowballs across the thick white carpet, and on reaching the *Rose and Crown*, had a pint or two before returning home. We had had the place to ourselves, except for one lonely publican.

Back home, we settled into armchairs by our open fire, and mentioned mince pies, when we heard the sound of an engine. In this weather? With significant drifts across the lanes? The engine stopped, and the doorbell rang.

"Hello", said the tall smiling figure, shaking off a dusting of snow. "I'm Philip, your local friendly farmer. Just calling in to introduce myself, and to offer milk, eggs, or anything else I can fetch you on my tractor". I am so thankful for this county, for tractors, and for the friendly people of rural Norfolk, of whom Philip and his wife Rona are two of the best.

And before the tractor? My memory took me back to the practice where I had first worked after qualifying. It was a Dorset town perched on top of a rather steep hill. Shaftesbury, previously Shaston (Roman), previously Palladwr (Saxon), is well known for Gold Hill, steep, cobbled and extremely picturesque. It was used in a well-known television advert for Hovis bread, and in a couple of scenes in the film *Far From the Madding Crowd* (1967). The practice owner told me that during the previous winter it had snowed incessantly for a few days, and that the town was totally cut off. He looked through his appointment book, and realised that all patients that day were from the surrounding villages, and would be unable to attend. Then the doorbell rang. He answered it to find a character resembling the abominable snowman standing there.

"Sorry I'm a little late", said the snowman. "I've tethered my horse to your gatepost. How long do you think I'll be. It's just a small filling I'm booked in for, I believe".

The main predecessor of the tractor was the horse. And the horse has been around for a long time. The most ancient remains of a horse in Britain were found in the county immediately south of Norfolk, namely Suffolk, at Pakefield. They are estimated to be from around 700,000 BC. At that time, horses were not used for riding or pulling, but were hunted for meat. It was not until 2,500 BC that they were domesticated and used for riding and towing carts. Riding a horse in those days was a skillful activity, as stirrups and saddles (and horseshoes) were not invented until the final 3 centuries BC. But by the time the Romans arrived in Britain, the various tribes could assemble thousands of horse-drawn chariots to do battle. Boudicca (or Boadicea, in Latin), was famous for her chariot with scythe blades attached to the wheels, and is described more fully in a previous volume (*Big Blue Sky*, 2022). Developing specific breeds for specific tasks took place in the 17th century, and agricultural equipment and machinery to be worked by horses was designed accordingly. But with the advent of the tractor, and the internal combustion engine, horses became increasingly redundant, and from the 1980s, have been used almost exclusively for recreational purposes.

"Do you know the Blackboys?" sounds almost politically incorrect these days. The *Blackboys Inn* is (not are) around 400 yards from my old dental practice in the town of Aylsham, and is an inn, with restaurant and rooms. And just 7 miles away, in the direction of Cromer, is another *Blackboys Inn* in the village of Aldborough. The name is said to be derived from Charles ll, who was nicknamed the black boy on account of his black hair and swarthy complexion. And although the Aylsham inn dates from 1471, it was not until the mid-17th century that it became a coaching inn.

The coach was a development of the cart, and in England, was developed a century or so later than in Europe. The reason for this was that our roads were little more than cart tracks. The early coaches were extremely uncomfortable to ride in, but later, in the mid-17th century, springs were used to counteract the bumpiness of the roads.

By the mid-18th century, there was a network of coaching routes across England, and hundreds of inns were spread out at 7 to 10 mile intervals. Coaching inns were built around an inner courtyard and stables, and tired horses were replaced with fresh ones, while the travelers could enjoy food, or stay and rest. Coaches were now travelling considerable distances over the course of a few days, and pulled by more than 2 horses. The *flying coaches* ran at around 8 mph, twice the speed of the everyday coach, and by the early 19th century, 12 mph was being achieved. And then the railways arrived, coaches became redundant, but the inns remained.

The coach would arrive at one of these inns every 2 or 3 hours. Bearing in mind the rattling and shaking of the coaches, the inns provided welcome relief for tired passengers. And it was not just the shaking, but also the dreadful stench. This was not due to the horses, but to the passengers. After some time, coaches had seats inside (for the gentry and others willing to pay the price), and a rear outside bench seat for the poorer, and assumed smellier, passengers. Coaching inns followed suit, and likewise had smart lounges for the more affluent patrons, and rather basic bars for the less privileged. Horses could be changed for fresh ones, or stabled overnight. For many people, this enabled travel from city to city, until... "Stand and deliver", cried the masked highwayman. In literature, he verges on being a romantic figure, but in reality, he was a 17th and 18th century bandit, terrifying and even murdering passengers on the coaches. If caught, he was hanged.

Coaching inns today abound across our county. Some have been modified or extended, and are generally listed buildings. The *Blackboys Inn* in Aylsham is just one fine example of their continuing hospitality. The menu is comprehensive, the meals served in more than ample portions, and for those wishing to stay, there are 8 *en suite* traditionally furnished, but modern, comfortable rooms.

The roads in our county can be quite an experience. When I was a lad, we were proud of our Norfolk dual-carriageway, which was probably one of the country's first. It meandered between the tiny villages of Tunstead and Scottow, and was two single-carriageway winding lanes, separated by a line of oak trees. It was signed as a dual-carriageway, and some would cite that as another example of *Normal for Norfolk*.

More recently, proper dual-carriageways have been constructed, and this has made access to and from the county much easier, both from London, especially, and from the Midlands, to some extent. But many of our local roads continue to wind around the periphery of every field. For two years I travelled 9 miles from Wroxham to North Walsham each schoolday on a yellow double-decker bus. That was in the 1950s. The girls were upstairs and the boys downstairs. A large bearded man stood by the stairs to make sure there was no mixing, as we snaked our way along lanes, including the afore-mentioned dual-carriageway. One day one of the rear tyres caught fire. Maybe it was flat and the driver had not noticed, but some of the lads did. No-one told the driver, or the bearded bouncer – it was too exciting, and no-one wanted to see it put out. Remarkably, only the tyre caught fire, and not the rest of the vehicle. At our destination, my schoolmates and I stood grinning, gazing at the burnt rubber and smoke. On another memorable occasion, the bus became stuck in a snowdrift, as recounted in an earlier volume (*Big Blue Sky*, 2022). The way this situation was handled would result in prosecution today, and I will return to it in a later chapter. Another memory of the school bus was when a crumpled note was smuggled down from the upper deck, maybe when the bearded bouncer was dozing. Sniggering first formers passed the note along to me, and I innocently opened it and read, 'I love you. Carol'. Who was Carol? Someone told me she was one of the Tunstead girls, and I peered through the steamed-up bus window when we stopped in that village, and wondered which one was Carol. I never found out. Soon after, our family moved to North Walsham and I walked to school each day. But for a long time, I decided that the name Carol was the prettiest name I had ever heard.

*******

"If she ain't leaking oil, it means she's run out!", said Harry Curtis, one of my farmer patients. He was speaking about his Land Rover.
"I was out in a field, searching for treasure with my metal detector, and guess what I found?" said another patient who resided in the county. "I found a Land Rover. It was a lovely *Discovery*!"

They were tongue-in-cheek, as these Land Rover jokes were as old as the hills. But this is Norfolk, where one probably sees even more Land Rovers than tractors. They used to be simply Land Rover, but these days one sees Freelander, Discovery, Defender, Range Rover Sport, and Range Rover Evoque, to name but a few. The older vehicles look almost as if they are constructed from one of the original Meccano kits, of small metal strips, nuts and screws, whilst the Evoque is streamlined, tasteful, and probably described as 'cool' by my grandchildrens' generation. But it all started with the Jeep.

Up until the year 1947, the only 4-wheel drive vehicle on the road was a Jeep. That year, Maurice Wilks, the chief designer of Rover cars, used the axles and chassis of a Jeep, and at his farm on the Isle of Anglesey, produced the first Land Rover. The Jeep had its steering wheel in the middle of the dashboard, and so did the Land Rover. It was described as 'centre steer'. He called it an off-roader, and it was a very agricultural piece of kit. He had a supply of surplus aircraft cockpit paint, and so it was painted military grey.

Farmers saw the potential, and sales took off. It was the first mass produced 4-wheel drive vehicle with doors. A hard roof was optional. Over the years, the wheel base got longer, and the engine became bigger and more powerful. The Range Rover was introduced in 1970, and was a very upmarket, luxury development of the agricultural models. The Defender was re-evaluated in the 1980s, when Japanese SUVs started competing with Land Rovers. The result was the Discovery, which was a very practical, versatile, but family-friendly vehicle. The Range Rover Evoque was introduced in 2011, and is described as a compact, luxury SUV. And it has style.

The late Duke of Edinburgh loved Land Rovers, and was gifted the 100th vehicle produced. He married Princess Elizabeth in 1947, the year Land Rovers were launched, and he took his vehicle on their Commonwealth tour of 1953. It was designed to enable them to stand and wave out of the back of the vehicle.

In January 2019, he came out of their Norfolk home, the Sandringham estate, in a Freelander 2, hit a passing Kia, and overturned his vehicle. At the age of 97, he stepped out of the Freelander unhurt, and the following day, was seen driving an identical model. The following month, he handed in his driving licence.

He decided to have a bespoke hearse, and collaborated with Land Rover to design the vehicle. He started the project at the age of 80, and took 16 years modifying a Defender. The late Queen modified the design further to give it an open back, and olive green paintwork.

Some days when driving, it seems that almost every other car on the road is a Land Rover of some description. Norfolk - a county of Land Rovers.

*******

Land Rovers might well be an integral part of the Norfolk landscape, but there is another vehicle that could not be more different, and yet is produced in the county. Like the Land Rover, it is recognised and used, or enjoyed, globally.

"I see you're supporting local industry, old chap!" Andrew stood in his front doorway grinning at me, as my wife and I virtually rolled, slowly, out of the white *Lotus Esprit* that I had just flung onto his drive. Lotus cars are produced just south of Norwich in the village of Hethel. Cars were discussed briefly over dinner, and in order to preserve the sanity of our wives, we tried to keep off the subject of teeth. Andrew had a dental practice in the city of Norwich, around a mile from mine.

I enjoyed the amazing performance, and riveting good looks of the car in those days. If we needed to travel as a family, there was my wife's estate car. But the Lotus was my everyday car, and led to a little humour more than once.

"Does your car go under water?" asked Billy, a teenager who had come to the surgery for his six-monthly examination. "I saw it on the screen at the Odeon last month. Just like yours. And I expect your name is Moneypenny", he said to my nurse, with a seductive wink. The James Bond film *The Spy Who Loved Me* (1977) had been released a year or so earlier, but this was Norfolk, where many things happen slowly. Bond's car in the film was a specially adapted white Lotus Esprit, and at one point in the story, he drives it off a jetty and into the sea, and submerges, whilst wing-like fins and a rudder appear. He launches a rocket from it to destroy one of the villain's helicopters, and comes ashore on a crowded beach. The Secret Service secretary, Miss Moneypenny, who invariably appeared in each Bond film, was not with him in the car.

"If you have an expensive car, don't hide it away. You might think patients will feel you earn too much, and be embarrassed, but it doesn't work like that". Reg, the practice owner where I was the newly qualified associate, had been on a dental course, and was excitedly telling me what he had learned. "Put your car where all your patients can see it. So they have to walk past it. So they almost trip over it. They'll think you're a successful dentist, and assume that you're good at what you do, and that people must pay a lot for your treatments. It sort of 'sets the scene'. Brings in people looking for some of the more sophisticated treatments we've been trained to carry out". A month or two later, Reg bought a new Jaguar, which took up residence on the drive at the front of the practice, next to his wife's MGC GT. His patients had to 'nearly trip over' two expensive cars to reach his front door. I left my rather elderly Ford Anglia a few hundred yards down the road, out of sight. And years later, I drove a Lotus Esprit. Had I seen it in the James Bond film? Actually, I had not seen the film, nor heard about it at the time. It was a bargain buy, a few months old, and already falling hugely in value. And for around 18 months, it was a lot of fun for a young middle-aged man.

Although I had not been very interested in cars as a boy, one could not help but notice some of the models driven by senior consultants at the hospital where I trained. A dark blue *E-type Jaguar* caused me to stop and catch my breath. It was the most beautiful car I had ever seen. Not far from where the Jaguar was parked stood a metallic silver *AC Cobra*, sleek and just oozing wild power. And there was a *Lotus Elan.* Lotus cars were rarely seen on the roads in those days, and when you did see one, it was nearly always an *Elan.* It was an elegant car, almost pretty. Later, the distinctive mid-engined *Europa* caught one's eye. But I loved my *Esprit* for the relatively short time I had it. A car produced in slow, sleepy, relaxing Norfolk - but a powerful beast with stunning looks.

*******

117

*Unfurled toilet paper streamed from the train's windows.*

The railway train from Sheringham came chugging into the station at North Walsham, and as it slowed, brakes started hissing and carriages shuddering. There appeared to be a celebration of some kind, with streamers flowing from many of its windows. Until closer inspection revealed that they were not streamers at all. They were unfurled toilet rolls! And later that morning, a number of my fellow pupils at the Paston School, who hailed from the towns of Sheringham and Cromer, were marched up to the headmaster's study, where they were invited to provide an explanation, before bending over a chair and atoning for their amusing display.

The railway system in Britain, and so many other countries in the world, was a result of the industrial revolution. The big railway boom was in the 1840s, with a multitude of independent local companies. The government took control of them during the First World War, and in 1923, they were amalgamated into 4 companies, known as the Big Four. In 1948, they were nationalised and became British Rail. In the late 1959s and 1960s, passenger numbers declined, as did profits, and Dr. Richard Beeching was brought in to make the railways profitable again. He axed innumerable lines, especially those serving rural communities, and in Norfolk, many countryfolk found their local stations closed and the lines taken up. 2,300 stations were closed, and many were in Norfolk. 5,000 miles of track vanished. Dr. Beeching's name became a virtual curse word amongst many rural people, who felt he had left them stranded in their villages.

'Muddle and Go Nowhere' was the name by which the M&GN, or *Midland & Great Northern* railway line, was known in Norfolk. It connected southern Lincolnshire with the Isle of Ely and North Norfolk. It was incorporated in 1893. The M&GN served a largely agricultural community in Norfolk, though there was an increasing surge in summer, due to the popularity of the region with holidaymakers. After 1945, and especially after nationalisation in 1948, it became increasingly unprofitable, and was closed in 1959. Today, just a small section between the Victorian holiday resort of Sheringham and the Georgian town of Holt (famous for Gresham School) is in service, as a heritage line, operated by the *North Norfolk Railway*. It is called the *Poppy Line*.

"Wow! A romantic evening dinner on the *North Norfolk Railway*. Look what my daughters have given me for Father's Day". And so Wendy and I drove to Sheringham, and joined others congregating on the platform, and peering through the windows, where every carriage resembled a restaurant. We could have been back in the 19th century. It was romantic, and it was also Norfolk.

"Are yer awlroight? Yer can board when yer loike", said a uniformed guard. We were shown to a table for two, reserved for us. A couple sitting opposite smiled, and we exchanged pleasantries. I felt I knew them, but was not sure. That's Norfolk. And then there was a whistle, the carriage gently jolted, and we slowly edged out of Sheringham station. It was early evening in November as we gazed out across wide fields, and were just about able to detect the sea through the twilight at times. If it had been early summer, we would have seen carpets of poppies in corn fields. We passed through woods, where shadowy deer were quietly foraging between the trees. It was magical. What a memorable evening.

"Yer get yer starter between Sheringham and Holt. Yer can get orf at Holt while we tunn the train round. Or yer can stay hair on board. Yer get yer main course between Holt and Sheringham. And yer can get orf again in Sheringham. We gart to git the engine to the other end, yer see. Then yer get yer sweet between Sheringham and Holt…" informed an appropriately decked out waiter, who like the rest of the team, was a local, unpaid, railway enthusiast.

"And we can get off again in Holt while you turn the train round. You take the engine to the other end, and pull us backwards, as it were?" I volunteered.

"Yer gart it, sir. And then yer have yer carffee between Holt and Sheringham".

"And then we go home", I concluded. Yes, I had got it.

And so we were wined and dined, backwards and forwards along the *Poppy Line*, attended by authentic looking staff, with the nostalgic smell of smoke in the air, and all the chugging and whistling that accompanied railway journeys in the days of my childhood. We alighted from the train a time or two whilst 'the train gart tunned round', and made conversation with a few other local folk. And late evening, feeling pleasantly mellow (though having imbibed little wine myself as designated driver for the two of us), we finally drew into Sheringham station for the final time. We bade farewell to the friendly couple who had sat opposite us for the duration of the evening, and drove home, vowing to recommend the adventure to all our friends.

Around 3 weeks later, a slightly larger than average envelope fell onto our doormat amidst the morning post.

Inside was a photograph of the two of us enjoying our main course on board the Poppy Line dinner evening. There was a brief note with it. *'I'm sure you knew that you knew me, but you could not place me, could you? Here is a photo of the two of you, with best wishes from your vet's nurse. Pam. And love to your cat, Bathsheba'.*

Occasionally today, with the wind in the right direction, we can just about hear the horn of trains on the *Bure Valley Railway*. The line was laid on the trackbed of the old *Great Eastern Railway*, where it ran between Aylsham and Wroxham. As a lad, I lived in Wroxham between 1953 and 1958. Later, from 1984 to 2002, I had a dental practice and book shop in the market town of Aylsham. The line opened in 1990. And so, for me, the *Bure Valley Railway* is on familiar territory, and from time to time, we take grandchildren, either from Wroxham to Aylsham to meet Father Christmas, or from Aylsham to Wroxham, where they have a summertime boat trip on the river Bure.

Norfolk County Council has a policy of retaining the trackbeds of former railways for use as footpaths, and alongside the 9 miles of the *Bure Valley Railway*, runs a footpath. I wonder if some of the 100,000 passengers a year recall scenes from the *Railway Children* broadcast on BBC television in 1957, of three children happily waving as the train passes? There has been a film and a remake since, but someone of my vintage recalls that atmospheric and memorable television series making its mark on our childhood. Wendy and I always wave to the trains.

So what do you do with land that was previously a railway track? As stated above, footpaths has been the answer in many parts of Norfolk, and elsewhere. Wendy and I love walking the county by using the old *M&GN* railway line. There are so many walks utilising the land that previously carried railway track. The *Norfolk Ramblers* are just one group that promote walking the old railway tracks. One of their walks involves passing 2 restored stations (now cafés), and meandering along Smugglers Way and Pudding Pie Alley, both in Reepham. Much of the walk is along *Marriotts Way*.

Wendy and I have been walking *Weavers Way*, in stages, village to village, for a number of years. The walks and views are stunning, and often involve the old *M&GN* railway track. The name *Weavers Way* suggests a well-worn track used by the Flemish weavers who fled here in the 14th century. But the walk is not historical in that sense, and is a compilation of various footpaths from Cromer to Great Yarmouth, and so named to commemorate the weavers who brought prosperity and identity to this region. At Cromer, the Weavers Way links with the *North Norfolk Coastal Path*, and at Great Yarmouth with the *Angles Way*. They join with *Peddars Way* to form a circuit around Norfolk. But without the old *M&GN* railway line, it is unlikely that so many charming rural walks would exist.

"Look at the ruins over there. This must have been Worstead station. I was a young lad a few miles away in Wroxham, and it would have been quite busy then. Now look at it". We were on one of our *Weavers Way* walks and had arrived at Worstead station. The small village of Worstead gave its name to worsted cloth, which was woven in the area by Flemish weavers during the Middle Ages. They brought great prosperity to the whole region. The large parish churches of Norfolk are a direct result of this industry, and are sometimes referred to as the Wool Churches. Our circular walk started by the huge and magnificent church in the tiny village of Worstead, and had taken us along lanes and footpaths, and the old *M&GN* railway line. We paused, and surveyed the site, imagining the quiet expectation of countryfolk waiting for the train to arrive, smoke billowing from its funnel, and then proceeding, maybe to Norwich, for a shopping spree. Or perhaps to Cromer, for a walk along the prom, and cod and chips served in a copy of the *Daily Mirror*. The ghosts had long gone. A blackbird gave its clack, clack, clacking alarm call, and other birds departed. Like the trains. And all was now quiet.

On another occasion, it was a Boxing Day walk, cold and icy, but under a big blue sky. Norfolk is sunny, but can also be cold. The wind is reputed to come straight from the Russian steppes. Others say the arctic. We walked along the main road in the village of Melton Constable, described by some as 'the strangest village in Norfolk'. The appearance of the terraced houses suggests that it has been plucked straight out of Derbyshire or Nottinghamshire. It owes its existence to the convergence of several *M&GN* railway lines - from Kings Lynn, Norwich, Cromer and Great Yarmouth. And so it was decided to create a village here, Victorian, with railway station, terraced houses for the railway workers, school, marshalling yards, iron foundry and gasworks. The village population grew from 118 in 1881 to 1,157 in 1911. But with the decline in the use of the railways in the mid-20th century, and the Beeching Axe of 1964, the station was demolished, and the railway area turned into an industrial estate. The overall atmosphere is that of a Victorian industrial town. Perhaps Dickensian characters such as Mr. Pickwick or Mr. Bounderby might come strolling down the street. And then one is suddenly out of the village, and walking the footpaths, fields and woods that are so typically Norfolk.

\*\*\*\*\*\*\*

"Yew can tell a black 'eaded gull easy", said the ranger, taking us around *Horsey Mere*, and the surrounding dykes. "It's got a brown 'ead!" We were on one of Ross' wildlife boat trips. It was so peaceful, and there was so much to see.

People have travelled along the Norfolk waterways for centuries, and for a variety of reasons. Until the late 19th century, it was mainly commercial. Today, the majority of those out on the water are using it for leisure.

Norfolk is a county famous for its water, especially the broads. But there is a long coastline, and there are a large number of rivers, and water transport, from Viking ships to local wherries, and from herring drifters to holiday cabin cruisers, have played a significant part in defining our county and giving it identity.

Viking raiders attacked and conquered northern and eastern England from the late 8th century through to the 11th century. In the mid-9th century, they stormed ashore at the area known as the Island of Flegg, at Scratby and Hemsby, and moved inland. They killed the East Anglian king Edmund (later canonized) at the battle of Hoxne, near Diss, sacked Thetford and burned Norwich. From Norfolk, they fought their way across East Anglia, and then west across England, until King Alfred the Great withstood the Viking Guthrum, and the Treaty of Wedmore brought peace in 886 AD. In general terms, Viking warriors then became Norfolk farmers. The village where I live was founded by a Viking, and many place names in Norfolk, are of Norse origin. Some examples are Pockthorpes (fairy settlements), Thwaite (clearing), Toft Monks (dwelling), and Winterton (headland). 'By' means settlement, and there are 13 villages with names ending in 'by'. Examples are Hemsby, Filby, and Thrigby. There are also Norse surnames, such as Grimmer.

The Vikings left their mark on the county in many ways, one of which is the distinctive Norfolk sailing craft, the wherry. The basic design is derived from the Viking ships. The mast is well forward and there is one huge gaff rig, with a single high-peaked sail. They were built in various sizes, according to the width and depth of the waters they were to be sailed in. They carried freight, and were known as trading wherries. But with the advent of railways in Victorian times, much of the freight was switched to rail transport, and as Norfolk was opening up for tourism, many became pleasure craft. Freight wherries were somewhat cumbersome for pleasure, though, and more streamlined wherry yachts were later developed. A few wherries have survived into the 21st century, and can be chartered from the *Wherry Yacht Charter Charitable Trust*.

The herring, a fish that existed in huge shoals, had a most significant influence on Norfolk. I have written about the drifter fleets, and of the trade and prosperity brought to Great Yarmouth, in a previous book (*Big Blue Sky*, 2022), but this was another example of waterborne vessels shaping the identity of the county. Today, the herring fleet has gone, and wherries are a rare sight, but there is no shortage of vessels bringing commerce and pleasure to our county of rivers.

\*\*\*\*\*\*

We set off early evening, gliding through the ethereal mist that hung over the surface of the water. The band continued playing, and a few hours later, folk leant over the rail, gazing at the reflected moonlight on the river surface. The bar was full of convivial chatter and laughter, and the supper tables were largely empty, as we sailed from Salhouse broad, and back to the village of Horning, from whence we had set sail a few hours earlier. The vessel was the *Southern Comfort*, which had the appearance of a Mississippi paddle boat. We had taken 97 guests out for the evening to celebrate Wendy's 60th birthday.

And along the way we saw a number of black-headed gulls. Do you remember how Ross, the ranger at Horsey, taught us to recognise them? Yes - they have brown heads! What a fascinating thing to know, that a black-headed gull could easily be distinguished by the fact that it has a brown head. Until another ranger, on a later occasion, taking us on a boat trip around Ranworth Broad, told us that black-headed gulls also have white heads for much of the year. Help!

Pleasure, sport, tourism and leisure are all words very much associated with the rivers and broads of East Anglia. However, life on the waterways of Norfolk reflects life on the land, with residential and commercial, as well as the obvious leisure. There are those who live on the water, often in house boats moored to the bank alongside others. That is their home, where they are based. They live there, with living room, kitchen, bedrooms. Usually a car is parked nearby, and life is similar to that of those living in conventional buildings, except they are afloat.

"Look over there. Anyone for an ice-cream?" It's red, white and blue, with a huge plastic ice-cream cone protruding from the bows. It's the Norfolk Broads Ice-cream boat. Our village is visited almost daily by an ice-cream van, heralded by the tinkling jingle of 'I do love to be beside the seaside', even though we are at least a 15 mile drive from the coast. But on or near Salhouse Broad, you will find the aquatic equivalent. There are moorings on the river Bure just outside the broad, and on a sunny summer day, the boat is usually tethered to one of the posts, with those of holidaymakers alongside. And the trade in 99s appears to be brisk. Other forms of commercial vessels include reed cutters supplying the material for the abundance of thatched roofs, and dredgers keeping the waterways as open as possible.

"Watch out. Police!" I have never seen a police boat with flashing lights and wailing siren, but they do have a presence on the water. There are rules that need to be adhered to, as on the highways. Boats sail on the right side of the waterway, and not on the left, unless a sailing boat is tacking (the technical term for zigzagging across the river in order to take advantage of a head wind). Then the sailing boat has the right of way, and everyone else has to take evasive action. There are also speed limits, because too much wash produced by a speeding boat can erode and destroy the river bank. For this reason there are small blue and white boats, with *POLICE* displayed on a small flag at the stern. There are times when a vessel has to pull over, and an enthusiastic young male holidaymaker receives a lecture on the rules of the waterways. And bearing in mind our recent legislation with regard to diversity and equality, I should add that perhaps the river police also chase old ladies speeding in high-powered speed boats along our rivers and across our broads. Having said that, there are also moments of drama, where a real chase along the water is involved. One case recently resulted from a domestic dispute on a boat, and involved a chase of a few miles, and there have also been suspicious deaths and murders on our county's waterways.

*******

"This is yer dooty free", said the corpulent, smiling Norfolk official (had he slept in his uniform?), with responsibility to look after those of us flying out from *Norwich Airport*. He opened a large cupboard, and beamed at us. "Oi've gart three brands of cigarettes, and Scartch whisky and other booze. And perfooms. Hev a look. Let me know what yer want". The whole experience was totally underwhelming, but within half an hour, we were led out across pasture, ascended metal steps into the aircraft, and in no time, were climbing up into that big blue sky.

That was in the early 1980s. I felt that Norwich airport itself could have been mistaken for a small agricultural complex set in the midst of pasture. But life and style were changing for our city's airport, largely due to the discovery of oil and gas at various sites off the eastern coast of the British Isles, and the need for those working the rigs to travel between sites. Flights to Aberdeen and Edinburgh increased, and more recently, charter flights to a plethora of European holiday resorts.

The current airport site was originally an *RAF* airfield, Horsham St. Faiths, built in 1939, although the first commercial airport serving the city was situated on Mousehold heath, and opened in 1933. The military airfield closed, and Norwich airport moved to the site in 1968, and became established during the 1970s.

129

CRASH! The still of the night was shattered by an explosion, and a fireball rose into the pitch black sky from the common beside my cottage in Frettenham. Lights came on in the few dwellings in the vicinity, and soon, villagers were rushing to the scene, shouting to one another in an attempt to save lives.

A lady in a bikini was painted on the fuselage, alongside the nickname of the plane itself - *THE BELLE OF BOSTON*. It was a B-42 Liberator, and it burned fiercely. Derek Hewitt and his father were some of the first at the scene, before ambulances and fire engines arrived, and pulled injured *USAF* airmen from the blazing wreck. Of the crew of 10, 3 were rescued and survived. The plane had taken off from Horsham St. Faiths airfield, an engine had caught fire immediately after take-off, and after skimming a few tree tops, an oak had torn off a wing. It crashed into the common beside the cottage that has been my home since 1983. That was the night of 8th May 1944, and today, Derek's son Trevor has a museum devoted to wartime air memorabilia. It is based at a previous garden centre in our village, is huge and comprehensive, and it was the crash of *The Belle of Boston* that inspired its founding.

"You can still see the notch in the oak tree", Trevor told me. "Just outside the village, on the road to Norwich. Past the bridge over the beck, up the hill, right side of the road. And that was nearly 80 years ago".

A legless legend had been Squadron Leader of *242 Squadron* just 7 miles away a few years earlier. Douglas Bader, later knighted, and who had lost both legs before the war in an aerobatic accident, had been stationed at *RAF Coltishall*. During the early years of the war, he was credited with shooting down 22 enemy aircraft, plus a number of possibles. He baled out over occupied France in August 1941, and was captured. He escaped from prisoner of war camps so many times, that the Germans eventually confiscated his artificial legs, and later incarcerated him in *Colditz Castle*, until it was liberated in 1945. *RAF Coltishall* continued as a base until 2006. Today, it is the site of a prison, *HMP Bure*, for sex offenders, and an industrial estate named *Badersfield*.

East Anglia, being flat and situated relatively close to the European mainland, was the site of many airfields during the second world war. There were 37 in Norfolk alone, a number originally being *RAF* stations but later being given to the *USAF*, before being returned to the *RAF* at the end of the war. Today, just one, *RAF Marham*, continues as a RAF base, where F-35 Lightnings, stealth fighters, are based. And the others? *RAF Hethel* was taken over by *Lotus Cars*, where the runways are ideal for speed trials, and *RAF Snetterton* has become a motor racing track. *RAF Langham* was bought by Bernard Matthews, and is a turkey farm, and *RAF Sculthorpe* became a base for atomic bombers during the Cold War. It is now largely a business park.

*******

From Viking ships to stealth fighters, and from Boudicca's chariot to Matt's tractor, Norfolk has seen a variety of forms of transport, and methods of travel, over the centuries. Stealth fighters and Lotus cars are at the cutting edge of their respective fields. But for many years, the bicycle was my preferred mode of transport, trundling along leafy lanes, pausing to admire our huge 'Wool' churches, and watching kestrels hovering whilst hunting over the road verges. For me 'Muddle and Go Nowhere', and *Normal for Norfolk* more accurately describe something of this county that I love. Now in my latter years, this country bor is more than happy to sip chilled white wine with his rustic friend Matt, his tractor parked on the drive, in a county that largely enjoys a slower and more relaxed pace of life.

# Chapter Five

## My Norfolk Char Ladies

*Evaporating sherry, poltergeists in the wardrobe, and
vanishing £1 coins*

Jean - and always known as 'Jean', and never as Mrs.
Scrimple - was reliable and efficient. She faithfully
appeared on the doorstep at 8am every Wednesday
morning before I left for my surgery. She was short,
shrew-like, bordering on emaciated, hollow-cheeked, and
with the aroma of stale fag ash. And when I returned for
lunch shortly after 1pm, the carpets had been vacuumed,
there was not a cobweb in sight, and the dining room air
was heavy with the fragrance of *Pledge* furniture polish.
There was however, a slight problem to Jean's visits, and
I was not sure how to address it - sherry evaporated. It
was a fact - whenever Jean passed through the house,
sherry evaporated. And from within the decanter!

\*\*\*\*\*\*\*

Jean was a char lady. Or charwoman. In fact, she was one
of many char ladies employed by me during the years I
have lived in my Norfolk village home.

The first *charwoman* appears in records of the Borough
of Nottingham in 1379, though the term was not widely
used until the 1590s. The word *char* is a corruption of
Middle English *cherre*, meaning 'turn of work', and
*chore* today is a corruption of char. A charwoman, or
char lady, is a lady who does casual domestic cleaning

*Whenever Jean passed through the house, sherry evaporated!*

work. They come in all shapes and sizes, and those who are efficient and reliable are like gold dust. Rather like ones small toe, a char lady can be taken for granted. But like the small toe again, if she is suddenly absent, her value is soon appreciated.

The better off people had maids, and probably still do. My maternal grandparents had two maids and a nannie. That was around a century ago. All lived in, and as Grandpa and Nana lived with their four children in a sizeable flat situated over the family business, there was plenty of work for the maids. And the nannie looked after the children, until they were all away at boarding school. Goodbye nannie. My parents never had maids or nannie, and nor did my wife and I. But we have had char ladies. And when Jean was around, the sherry evaporated.

The fact that I kept a decanter of sherry at home, tends to date the story. "Drop in for a sherry", was a way in which one showed friendship, reached out to favoured strangers, or simply demonstrated social acceptance in the mid-1970s. I kept sherry in the consulting room at my city practice, and in a modest drinks cabinet in the sitting room at home. Sherry was a multifunctional tool - and sometimes the function was unconventional and unexpected. In the case of a certain nervous, if not petrified, if not near paralysed patient, named Clara Murphy, sherry proved to be the impromptu, acceptable and proficient answer to her problem, even if I would probably be struck off the dental register today. Clara had not been to a dentist for years, and was terrified of needles. Having heard me speak at a social function, she decided that I might possibly be worth a visit. She made it to the front door of the practice, but when I came to greet her, she fled. Sometime later, with unbearable pain from a wisdom tooth, a friend drove her to the practice, and virtually frogmarched her up the stairs to my consulting room. She was severely agitated, and was adamant that she would not accept any injections. Suddenly, I had a brainwave. Sherry. Not the perfect anaesthetic, but an effective tranquilliser and sedative. One tumbler full, and twenty minutes later, Clara could not care less about needles, opened wide for three injections, had the offending wisdom tooth removed, and left with the hint of a smile on her face. Well, one side of her face. Three cheers for sherry.

Retired GP, Dr. William Mather, another patient at my city practice, told me that sherry was 'jolly useful stuff'. "I spend summers here in my Norfolk home", said the doctor, "and winters in my Portugal villa. My wife and I enjoy meeting people, and we have our little social gatherings. In Norfolk, and in Portugal. And here's a word of advice, young man - when people arrive, put a glass of sherry in their hand. They don't have to drink it, though they usually do. But with a glass of sherry in their hand, the party's started, so to speak. And they relax, and start talking to each other. Try it! Works every time. Sherry".

I wonder if Jean, the char lady, shared Dr. Mathers sentiments? 'Dusting. Vacuuming. Cobwebbing. Polishing. Makes you ache. So, let the sherry evaporate. Just a small amount. Works wonders. Works every time. Sherry'.

It certainly evaporated. Or just went missing. I suspected something was amiss when I needed to top up the decanter sooner than anticipated. On several occasions. And so I measured the level in the decanter, 'before Jean' and 'after Jean'. I am not good at confrontation, and told myself it was all part of her pay. I was pleased with the way she looked after the house, and she was satisfied with her pay, including the sherry. Thank you Mrs. Scrimple - I mean, Jean - for looking after my cottage during my days as a single man.

*******

Enter Mrs. Northby. Though I cannot remember when Mrs. Northby first appeared. During my days as a toddler, and then as a child, she was always there. Well, once a week, and always had been. Surely every home had a Mrs. Northby.

She lived in a small thatched cottage at the end of the high street. To a five year old boy, it was simply 'where Mrs. Northby lives'. It was, in fact, a sixteenth century listed building, though it had seen better days. The roof was years overdue for renewal, and the rooms were small and dark. There was no electricity, and so no wireless, and when televisions started appearing some years later, no television. We left the village in the early 1950s, and shortly after, and purely coincidentally, an uncle and aunt, and in time, three of my cousins, arrived. That was over seventy years ago, but they still reminisce about Mrs. Northby's house. "No electricity, no lights, no radio, no television, and no mains water". However, there was a communal stand pump in a little courtyard, and Mrs. Northby and the residents of adjoining cottages collected their water from the pump. Quaint? More like Dickensian, but for Mrs. Northby and her neighbours, just the normal routine of life in post-war Britain, and no different than her parents had known.

"She's so superstitious", said my mother. Superstitious? What's that?, thought young Barrie. "If a black cat crosses her path, she is convinced that something bad will happen to her. So she waits until something bad *does* happen - then blames the cat", added mother.

"My young niece has been out picking May blossom", said Mrs. Northby, leaning on her broom and chatting away to my mother, alluding to the hawthorn that was in flower at that time of year. May. "It's so unlucky to bring it into your home. You just don't know what will happen if you do. Never have May blossom in your home, I always say".

Indeed, hawthorn blossom provokes more superstition involving 'bad luck', than any other plant or flower in the U.K. But I love it, though it has never occurred to me to bring it into the home. To my mind, there is something beautifully English about May blossom. I remember my first encounter so clearly.

I was in my late twenties, and having worked as an associate in another man's practice in Dorset, had bought my first dental practice in 1973 in Norwich. There was a rather shabby waiting room, and the equipment in the surgery looked medieval by today's standards. However, there was a shortage of dentists in the city at that time, and when word got round that a young chap was welcoming new patients, *and* treating them under the National Health Service, there was a veritable stampede in my direction. Rickety waiting room chairs, and instruments that might have looked at home in a blacksmith's forge, were ignored, "cos he's doin' it on the 'ealth service". The huge volume of patients resulted in a substantial turnover, which enabled refurbishment. That in turn drew in more patients than I could possibly have looked after, and resulted in the addition of a further four surgeries, waiting rooms, and a branch practice that was initially so small that I called it a 'twig practice' -

until it grew like the first one. Another story in another book. And in the early days, the two mile journey to and from work each day was covered on a yellow racing bicycle, which took me over a heath.

I always think of Norwich as a rural city. The expression 'rural city' is an obvious oxymoron, but people understand. Norwich is relatively small, as cities go. There is no heavy industry, the air is clean, one can reach countryside by driving less than fifteen minutes in any direction, and mooching around the city centre, lanes or open market, I usually meet people I know. There is a strong sense of community. And every boy and girl, from an early age, has seen cows, horses, sheep and pigs, which is not the case with children living in some of the country's larger, more industrialised metropolises.

During my early childhood, we lived some distance from Norwich, and I don't suppose that Mrs. Northby had been to Mousehold Heath. Or heard of it. Nor had I. It is an area of nearly two hundred acres of woodland and open heath on the north-east of Norwich. Until the nineteenth century, Mousehold was a much larger area, extending almost to the broads, and was maintained as heath by grazing animals and human supervision. During the nineteenth century, enclosures were developed, and other areas became farmland, or more recently, have been developed into housing, as Norwich expands, devouring innumerable acres of land, and the surrounding villages grow ever larger. But in the early 1970s, one feature of Mousehold Common was a bespectacled, curly-haired young man, careering along footpaths and bridleways on a yellow racing bicycle, morning and evening. And in late spring, there were times when his lungs suddenly filled with the most heavenly fragrance. I felt harmlessly intoxicated by it, and was left wondering from whence it had emanated.

Many years later, in 1983, I bought a small cottage on the outskirts of the village of Frettenham, a few miles north of the city. It was surrounded by a high hedge, and the following May, I found myself reliving those earlier days on the yellow racing bicycle. I was learning a few things about country life; it was April when much of the hedging burst into great clusters of white flowers, blackthorn, on leafless stems. There was little fragrance, and in the autumn, I failed to associate the blue-black fruit that was crushed underfoot, with the earlier blossom. Nor did I realise that *sloes*, as they are called, the fruit of the blackthorn, are famed for their use in the production of sloe gin. But I have learnt a thing or two over the years.

"Wow! Just one stem is more than enough", said Wendy, stripping the gleaming blue-black damson-like fruit from the proffered cutting, removed from the hedge with our trusty secateurs. For the first year or two in my cottage, the small plummy fruit that lay on the rear lawn, was trodden on, squashed, and passed largely unnoticed. Neighbours Bob and Lynn invited me round for dinner followed by sloe gin, my first Christmas here in Frettenham. Great neighbours, and a great liqueur. That was forty years ago. And now, we too have gone into production of the heavenly nectar. The hedge is weighed down with thickly stacked fruit, the like of which I have not seen before. We could start a factory. "Looking forward to Christmas", says Wendy with a wide smile.

All you need, in addition to 450gm of sloes, is 225gm of castor sugar, and a large sterilised jar. And gin! Wash the sloes and freeze them. Place the frozen sloes in the jar, and pour the gin, and then the sugar, onto them. They will thaw and the skins will split. Seal the jar, and shake vigorously. In fact, shake it every other day for a week, and once a week for 2 months. Then enjoy the dark red liqueur, perhaps poured over ice ('on the rocks'), or drizzled over ice-cream. I do enjoy country life – and Christmas!

I digress. If the blossom of the blackthorn was spectacular, a month later it was surpassed by great snowdrift-like swathes of cream-coloured flowers, covering other sections of the hedges. Whereas the blackthorn was on otherwise naked branches, this display of blossom was on leafy stems. And the fragrance was intoxicating, sweet, fresh and spring-like. Some describe it as vanilla, almond, or simply spicy. I would mooch around the garden, and find the temptation to thrust my face into clusters of the blossom, and inhale deeply, simply irresistible. I suspect that Mrs. Northby, however, would have taken several steps back. Country folklore may consider that hawthorn hedges are the homes of fairies, but her overwhelming sentiment was that May blossom was bad luck. Don't touch it. Don't bring it into your home. Stay away.

"I must confess that I love the smell of the May", Mrs. Northby confided in my mother, "but I'm not going to risk bringing bad luck into my home. I've heard too many stories of what's happened to folk who did. I'll just smell it from a distance, and leave it alone".

So Mrs. Northby did not bring May blossom into her home. Two weeks after that conversation, her brother died.

"And if you had brought the blossom into your home, you would have been mortified when your brother died. You would have blamed yourself for his death", my mother told Mrs. Northby. But she continued to repeat the folklore warnings, and kept her distance from the fragrant white blossom. She was a countrywoman, and rural superstitions and folklore had always been a part of her life. Mrs. Northby would not be taking chances.

And a foot-note on hawthorn. It was November 2008, and Wendy and I had just arrived in Argentina. It was our first time there, and it was spring. November. Southern hemisphere. A minibus had been waiting at the airport for us and our four companions. It was dusk, almost dark, and we could just make out that we were driving through countryside, eventually arriving at a small boutique hotel. And then, for me, the big surprise. Stepping out of the vehicle, my lungs filled with the beautiful fragrance of hawthorn blossom. It was like being back in Norfolk. *Crataegus monogyna* is native in the northern hemisphere, in Europe, Asia and North America, but has been introduced into many other countries. And even in New Zealand (and you can't travel much further than New Zealand) it is possible to inhale the beautiful bouquet of May. Even if it's November.

*******

Enter Mrs. Lambe. "Oi clean boots, I dew", she told my mother. This was to constitute part of our steep Norfolk learning curve. Born, bred and married in Norfolk, she lived just a few doors up the road from our home. (The unadopted, untarmaced road sloped down to our house, at the bottom of a *cul de sac*). In a previous tome I have written of how her accent had my mother totally bemused. "She doesn't just clean people's homes during the week, but on Saturdays, she cleans boots. Not shoes. Not any other items of clothing. She says she just cleans boots. How very strange. Boots!" And only when mother pressed Mrs. Lambe, did the mystery unfold. "Crooser boots, sailing boots…". and in fact, any boats that had been hired out for the week, or fortnight, on the local river Bure, and Norfolk Broads.

Mrs. Lambe. As with Mrs. Northby, we never found out her Christian name, which was unusual for char ladies. We knew her daughters' names - Sylvia and Lulu. They were in their late teens, and whereas the rather plain Sylvia was hardly noticed as she sauntered to catch the bus at the top of the road, Lulu's sylph-like figure, mini skirt and plunging neckline did not pass unobserved. My mother described her clothing as 'disgusting', though I always felt this was in some part a reaction to my father's obvious fascination with the girl!

My father's work had taken us out of the county for a few years, and Mrs. Lambe was my parents' first char lady following our return in the early 1950s. She was largely responsible for educating us with regard to the Norfolk accent. And the language - she used a dwile. In Norfolk, a dwile is a floor cloth, derived from the Dutch word for floor cloth, *dweil*. Along with Dutch barns, Dutch gables, and many surnames, Norfolk has been significantly influenced by Dutch culture.

Every char we have employed has been truly appreciated, and has ticked the boxes with regard to efficiency, punctuality, and a degree of respectful friendship. But there have also been occurrences that have caused me to raise my eyebrows.

\*\*\*\*\*\*\*

"Darling, I'm sure someone's been trying some of my frocks on. Or there's a poltergeist with a penchant for smart summer dresses hiding in our bedroom", said my wife. "I hang them on the wardrobe rail, all facing the same way. Well, I thought I had. Maybe I was in a hurry. But I think they are in a different order too".

Evelyn was a lady I met from time to time within the friendly community of the town where I worked, and a regular customer of my book shop. "If you ever need a cleaner, I have worked for a lot of people here in the town. I really enjoy it too", she volunteered.
"I'll let you know, if we need someone", I replied.
"Sorry", Evelyn said. "Can you speak up please. I'm a little bit deaf".

After a few years, Jean became a full time pensioner. I remembered that Evelyn had told me of her cleaning experience, and took her on to be cleaner in my village home. In fact, *we* took on Evelyn, because I had married since Jean had retired. All was well for a few months, and then, one morning, having left home for the surgery, I realised I had left my brief case back at the cottage. I turned the car round, and quickly drove back. Not only could I not get in, but it sounded as though someone was holding a disco in my home. The doors were locked, with keys inserted from within - so I could not unlock them, front or back. I rang the front door bell, and then rang the back door bell, but to no avail. I hammered on the door. I shouted. And I gave up. I could not get into my own home. When I reached the surgery, I telephoned home, but there was no reply.

My wife, who had left home before me, was receptionist and practice manager at my county surgery, where I was working that morning.

"She did say she's rather hard of hearing", she responded when I told her of my frustrating attempts to get into our home.
"I would be very hard of hearing if I lived with such decibels. I would probably be stone deaf in a week or two", I muttered.

So my wife went home early, waited on the drive until Evelyn emerged, and told her of my abortive attempts to get into my own home. Evelyn was clutching a ghetto blaster. She asked my wife to repeat what she had said, and then explained.

"If anyone came into the house while I was working, I wouldn't hear them. I'm a bit deaf, you see. So I lock the doors and leave the keys in. Very secure. And sorry about the music your husband heard. I love music while I work, and bring my music machine with me. Probably a bit loud for some though. Sorry. I'll turn it down in future".

My wife thanked her, and as she walked up the drive, Evelyn looked back and said, "By the way, I'm going to a wedding next month. Could I borrow your pretty green dress with the yellow flower pattern please? Just for the weekend. Fits a treat, it does".

I felt this was being intrusive. More than intrusive. Invasive in fact. Cheeky. But my wife told me that Evelyn was a really lovely and honest lady, and did not mean to be forward. Norfolk is friendly and we are village people. Of course she could borrow the dress.

145

Besides, they were the same size. But I still felt a little put out, and took some A4 sheets of paper, and wrote *NOSEY!* on them. The message was simple and straightforward, and I pinned them to the dresses inside the wardrobe door. '*NOSEY!*' Poltergeists don't like such posters, and the dresses remained on their hangers after that, and did not turn round anymore. And Evelyn was pleased to attend a wedding wearing a well-fitting green dress with a yellow flower pattern.

*******

"Oi foind it hard work cleaning yer house, so sometimes Oi go oot inter yer gaarden and Oi sit under yer wa'er sprinkler". (I find it hard work cleaning your house, so sometimes I go out into your garden, and I sit under your water sprinkler.)
It was summer, and it was hot, but surely she wasn't serious.
"You *are* joking", I retorted. "You don't really sit on the lawn under the sprinkler, do you?"
"Oi dew. Its refreshin'. And Oi soon droi out in the sunshine". (I soon dry out in the sunshine.)
"Cors she dew", said husband Simon. "As if she ain't wet enough anyway!"

Simon and Sylvia were relations. Not close relations. Family really, but not close family, strictly speaking, and certainly not Wendy's. And nor mine. (Work it out!). I am trying to be truthful, and yet obscure and vague. I want to preserve anonymity, but I want to tell you the story. It's true, and it's Norfolk. And it cost me a few hundred pounds - and a lot of heartache.

Evelyn's husband had become sick, and she felt she should be at home to look after him. "It's been coming on a long time, and now I really need to be with him all the time", she said.

"W' blust. Me and moi Sylvie can clean yer 'ouse for yer", said fairly obscure relation Simon, whom we were visiting shortly after Evelyn had announced her termination of employment. They had done it before. They did it in their own home. They could easily do it for us too. They had plenty of time on their hands, as they were self-unemployed. Sorry, correction - 'out of work'. We were obscure relations, if not family, and so they did not need paying. Maybe the occasional spot of cash, if that was OK with us, but they would love to help us out.

And so, every Wednesday morning, each week, Simon and Sylvia would arrive, presumably shortly after we had left for work, and when I returned from the surgery for lunch, the carpets were clean, the dining room smelled of polish, no cobwebs were in sight, and the twenty pounds I left for them in an envelope on the worktop had vanished. The dynamic duo had done their stuff.

It was about this time that I started a little financial project, with a short holiday break away in view. As a dentist, my income was more than adequate. And especially with seven surgeries at my city and county practices. However, some years earlier, my first marriage had failed, and in addition to the grief and heartbreak this brought me, I was left being financially responsible for my ex-wife and four children, who continued to live in the former family home. But I loved them dearly, and looking after them was a priority. And then, in the midst of the emotional chaos and turmoil, I had a clear call from heaven to open a Christian bookshop. It was an impossibility, both financially, and also in view of my impending divorce. However, I serve a God Who

"Sometimes I go out into your garden and sit under your water sprinkler", said Sylvia. "You *are* joking", I retorted.

specialises in impossibilities, and towards the end of 1984, *Sonshine Christian Bookshop* duly opened in the town of Aylsham, situated beside my dental practice there. A newspaper began an article with the words, 'In Aylsham, Norfolk, heaven and hell exist side by side', and I started to introduce myself to people with the words, "I am a man who sells holy books, and who fills holey teeth". I did not expect to make a profit (though it would have been welcomed), and my expectation was realised. The shop was an absolute joy, with lovely customers, fantastic staff, and a sense of doing really worthwhile work. But it lost an average of a little under £6,000 for each of its twenty years. No complaints - it was my pleasure to support my estranged wife, and my gorgeous daughters, and the bookshop, even if I had later remarried, and had another wife and home to look after. But my outgoing expenses were finely balanced against my income, and a little financial project might enable a weekend away some time.

"Take care of the pennies, and the pounds will take care of themselves", was an adage my mother taught me from an early age. And so I had been taking care of pennies and other small change, and putting them into a little pot. When enough coins had accumulated, I would replace them with a one pound note. Obviously, one pound was worth a lot more then than it is today (one pound in 1986 would be worth a little more than three times that, at the time of writing, 2023). I would wait until I had, say, £5, and then buy a National Savings certificate for that value. The interest rate was quite low, but if I cashed it in before it matured at perhaps three or five years, then I received no interest at all. That was the advantage, motivating me not to cash it in prematurely. And then, after three or five years, the proceeds would be encashed and reinvested. It helped get me through a challenging time, while making a small provision for the future. A few years later, in 1988, the government withdrew one pound notes, and replaced them with one pound coins. And around the same time, someone gave me a money box. It was pottery, and in the form of a letter box. The slot would receive coins of all denominations, but I felt that it was especially inviting for the new one pound coins.

Every evening, I checked the change in my pocket. The shrapnel was removed, and any pound coins popped into the money box. Also, I kept a count of how many coins had been fed into my pottery monster. One hundred! I resisted the temptation to use them for a restaurant trip, and continued feeding the box. Two hundred - one night by the sea? Resisted. The months passed. Three, four, five hundred, and that short break in a decent hotel continued to be resisted. Deferred gratification. But when I reached six hundred pounds, which had been fed into the box slowly over two years or more, those few days in a luxury hotel, with room overlooking the sea, and first-class restaurant, could no longer be delayed. Besides, we deserved it. The money box was placed on the dining room table, and the screw-top lid removed. The coins were tipped onto the tabletop, and amounted to... one hundred and fifty-six pounds. Impossible. I had recorded every coin, and I had collected just over six hundred. Horror! Our break away would not - could not – take place. And so what had happened to the missing four hundred and forty-four pound coins? Surely not. No way. They could not, could they? – they were sort of relations. And yet, what other explanation could there be?

Cunningly, I set a trap. One hundred and fifty pound coins were placed in the money box. I went to the surgery, Simon and Sylvia duly arrived and cleaned the house, and went home. I returned for lunch, and counted the coins. One hundred and forty-six. And so, the following week I placed one hundred and forty-five coins in the box, and after Simon and Sylvia had cleaned for the morning, there were one hundred and forty-two pounds. Just three or four pounds a week. Sometimes more? But they were relations. Family. They were trusted. Well, had been.

I came home mid-morning the following Wednesday, and there were Simon and Sylvia busy with their dusters. "Long appointment cancelled. So I'm home for a coffee. Would you like one?"

We sat together and discussed the weather, and Norwich City Football Club. And then I told them that I was a disappointed man. I had been collecting pound coins. "Have you noticed that money box in my study? Shaped like a letter box? I've been putting pound coins in there for months". They sat listening in silence. "Made a note whenever I put one in. Knew just how many were there". Their gaze fell, as they started taking interest in the floor. "I opened the box two weeks ago. Should have been six hundred pounds. But do you know what there was?" Silence from Simon and Sylvia, while they looked more intently at the floor, studying the pattern on the carpet. "One hundred and fifty-six pounds! Either I can't add up, or four hundred and forty-four pounds has vanished. *Four hundred and forty-four pounds*! Gone. And my wife and I cannot have the short break we have looked forward to".

I said no more, and Simon and Sylvia were clearly uncomfortable. But the coins stopped vanishing, and a few weeks later my cleaners, relatives, family, informed me that they had been offered cleaning work nearer their home, and would not be coming to my cottage any more. So there were no bad feelings within the family. They had got the message. They would never be in a position to repay the money, because they spent every penny as soon as they received it. I cut my losses in the interest of keeping peace within the family. Cleaners. Norfolk. But I guess that could happen anywhere.

However, would their next employer provide a garden sprinkler under which Sylvia could sit and cool off in the summer?

*******

About this time, I took on a couple to look after my city practice. Steve and Karen Brown. They had been patients for several years, though they did not see me professionally. I had five surgeries at that practice; there was a suite of surgery, waiting room and office/consulting room for me, and my associates and hygienists worked in the others. The Browns were patients of one of my associates.

"They're the salt of the earth", said my receptionist. "Decent people. Honest. Hard working, and Norfolk. They work days, but would appreciate a little extra cash. Evening work. And they're almost on our doorstep. Live in Junction Road, next to the practice". Karen worked at Startrite Shoes, and her children always had elegant footwear. Steve worked at Caley's chocolate factory, and was overweight and had bad teeth. They were in their late forties, and with the children having left home, would appreciate some extra pocket money.

And now a digression. A Norfolk digression. Albert Caley came to Norwich in the 1850s, probably because his brother, Nathaniel, a silk merchant, already lived in the city and had a business there. Albert opened a chemist shop in London Street, and started making drinks in his cellar - mineral waters that apparently had an exceptional taste. Demand increased, and Albert took on more staff, and moved to Bedford Street, and later to Chapelfield. Business was brisk in the summer, but cooled off in the winter. So Albert started producing cocoa in the winter months, and then chocolate. The latter was produced all year round, using milk from cattle at nearby Whitlingham. Business boomed, and in 1890, Albert built a factory that would employ hundreds, and send sweet fragrances into the Norwich air.

After Albert died, his son continued the business, and in 1904, A J Caley and Son were employing 700 people, and producing mineral waters (consumed by the royal family, and members of the Houses of Parliament), chocolates, and Christmas crackers. Their posters were designed by a young artist, Albert Munnings. They produced 40,000,000 chocolate eggs each Easter. But after nearly a century, and several takeovers, the factory closed in 1996, with hundreds of Norwich employees being made redundant. However Steve was still working at Caley's when he and Karen started evening cleaning in the late 1970s.

They really fitted the bill, being punctual, proficient, friendly and flexible. If one of the dentists was working late, they would work round him. Clean that surgery last. Or come back later, because "We only live round the corner. No trouble". Most of all, they were reliable. If one was ill, the other still came, and worked longer.

I have always liked to maintain good relationships with staff, patients, technicians… everybody. And in order to do that, I have usually taken the initiative. Staff were taken out for lunch periodically. Dentists who worked for me were taken out to dinner at a restaurant every few months, or came to our home. And everyone, including technicians and reps and cleaners, came to our Christmas lunch. We were professional, but we were friendly, and bonded together as a team.

One evening, I was driving home after a squash match, and realised that I would be virtually passing the Brown's home. I guessed they would have returned from their cleaning expedition, and sure enough, they answered my knock at the door, and said, "Hello Mr. Lawrence. We're just in from cleaning your place. Cup of tea? Have you got time?"

A brief visit, a cup of tea together, a short discussion concerning recent changeable weather (isn't it always?), the chances of Norwich City football team being relegated (been there before too), and of Callaghan's lack lustre style as prime minister, would pay dividends in good will. And help me to appreciate them more fully as the decent people I knew them to be. And then it was time to leave, but also, I was feeling increasingly uncomfortable. Squash is an energetic and exhausting game, and following the match earlier that evening, I had consumed two pints of lemonade. No - three pints.

"I ought to be going. Like to read the children a story before they go to sleep. But could I just use your loo before I go?"
"Of course", said Steve. But did I catch a change of expression on Karen's face, and had she just shot him a glance?
"Well, er, actually it's not at its best just now. The loo, that is. Wait till you get home", stammered Steve.

But the pressure within me was increasing by the second. "I've had a few pints of lemonade at the squash club. Getting a bit desperate".

"Nice car. You'll soon be home", added Steve quickly, and walking towards the front door.

"Really sorry Steve. I *need* your loo. I'm about to burst". Karen looked at Steve and shrugged her shoulders. Steve looked glum, and said, "First door on the left off the hall".

With an urgent pain in the nether regions, my gait spoke volumes as I walked quickly but awkwardly to their bathroom. More volumes! And a few minutes later, relief. I could relax again. I washed my hands, and turned toward the towel rail. I paused. There was something familiar about this place, though I had never been here before. It was a home from home. But why? Suddenly, having spent a penny (several), the coin dropped, so to speak. They used the same towels that I did. And quite a lot of them. Same colours and patterns. Same towels. Not like my home towels, but identical to the practice towels. But wait a minute... Steve had been so keen I should *not* use their bathroom, but there was nothing wrong in there. And Karen had given him the look. The towels. They were *my* towels. They had nicked them. Decent, salt-of-the-earth Steve and Karen had nicked my towels. I paused and considered. They were decent people. They were reliable, punctual and efficient (towel-nicking) cleaners. In every way, apart from the towels, I was pleased with them. And did I really want to lose them?

I emerged from the bathroom, and re-entered the sitting room. Silence. Steve and Karen were slumped in their respective armchairs, with Steve staring through the ceiling and Karen staring through the floor.

155

"That's better. Thank you so much, and for the tea. It's good to get to know one another. And now for home".

"Er, thanks. Um, really pleased to work for you. See you again", said Karen. They still looked quite worried.

"I really appreciate you looking after the place. By the way, loved your towels. Not quite the same as mine, I think, but similar. We all have the same good taste". I lied to them. "Take care. Enjoy the rest of the evening".

I suspect that I might also have been short of the odd bar of soap or roll of loo paper. But then again, I also suspected that they would be more careful in future. And I was pleased to retain two people who, in so many ways, *were* the salt of the earth.

*******

I had no real problem with those who had cleaned home and surgeries, but at one point, there seemed to be no one available. My home is not small, and with Wendy and me both working, a cleaner was more than necessary. And so I engaged a contract cleaner. But which?

*Ready Maid Services* immediately seemed attractive to me (I can't think why), as did *Meticulous Maids* and *Maid in Norwich*. But the price had to be as attractive as the company name, and I eventually opted for *Squeaky Clean Ltd*.

"I'm Stan. Pleased to meet yer. Now let's 'ave a gander at yer premises", said the proprietor, who clearly came from outside the county. South. London.

"Pleased to meet yer. Now let's have a gander at yer premises", said Stan.

Stan was short, overweight and sweaty. His light grey suit was a trifle tight, but he seemed to know a thing or two about cleaning houses.

"All girls fully trained by yours truly. Good girls, they are, and I keep 'em on their toes. Spot checks. I just call in and make sure they're doin' it proper. We're the kiddies. Trust me". Not a professional presentation exactly, but I would reserve judgement. I handed over a house key, and details of our security system.

Returning home after their first session, I was more than satisfied with the cleanliness of my home. After a month, I was satisfied that *Squeaky Clean* had been a good choice.

"Bad news", said my receptionist, entering the surgery at 11am one morning. "Your next patient has just cancelled. Taken ill at work. You're now free until after lunch".

There may have been no work in the surgery for the rest of the morning, but there was always paperwork (and computer work) that needed attention. After a quick coffee with my associate dentist, and a quick catch-up with my book shop manager next door, I drove home. Parking on the drive, I felt that all was not well. Two other vehicles were there, a years old Mini, and a rather snazzy red sports car. And the sitting room curtains were drawn.

The front door was locked, but as I turned the key, the sitting room curtains swished back. I strode through the hall and into the sitting room, where Stan and a young lady were sitting on the mat in front of the grate.

"And this is the brush, and this is the shovel, and I'll show yer 'ow to clean the fireplace proper", said *Squeaky Clean* Stan, red-faced and looking generally uncomfortable. "Just training up a new employee. Shows promise, don't yer Mandy".

From where I stood, Mandy was showing more than promise, with her plunging neckline and rather brief miniskirt. Peering out through heavy mascara, she smiled with glistening scarlet lips, and mumbled, "Oi dew moi best, Stan".

"So yer sweeps the ashes up wiv the brush, like, and into the li''le shovel, like, and then yer tips them into this plastic dustbin bag". Crouched together on the hearth rug, they both stared intently at the ash. And the brush. And the shovel. Maybe she was a slow learner, and perhaps he paid much attention to detail, but I suspected my arrival had interrupted something rather more intimate than learning to clean a fireplace.

"Why were the curtains drawn?" I enquired. There was silence as Stan started thinking.

"Cos the sun is bright, and was giving Mandy a headache. Didn't it, Mand? But it's not so bright now, and you're feeling be''er, aren't you Mand?"

"Yes Stan. Oi feel much be''er now. Thank yew Stan".

I explained that I had paperwork to do in my study, and would be at home until after lunch time. Stan handed his trainee a feather duster, with the words, "Go find some cobwebs, Mand", as he continued brushing, shovelling and bagging ash from the hearth. Around half an hour later, I heard two cars heading up the drive, out through the gate, onto the lane, and away.

I completed my paperwork, including a letter to *Squeaky Clean*, terminating their contract.

*******

I sold my city practice in the late 1980s, and my county practice in 2002, before retiring from dentistry in 2007. My previous wife had engaged a lady who lived in the village, and who was happy to be known as Mrs. Mop. I had vaguely met her through her husband. I had advertised in the village shop (since closed), for a garden roller to rent. Reg phoned and said I could borrow his for as long as I wanted. I rolled it noisily along Post Office Road, and kept it for so long that Reg could not remember to whom he had lent it. So he advertised the fact in the village shop, and I noisily rolled in back along Post Office Road. And then, many years later, Mrs. Mop arrived, and reminded me, laughing, "Yew were the one that had my Reg's roller". Village life - I love it.

I married Wendy in 2003, and after retiring, she became wife/cleaner and I was husband/cleaner. But the novelty soon wore off, and we engaged Rosemary, who is worth her weight in gold. Having lived in the village all her life, with her father looking after the post office (since closed) for decades, she knows everybody and everything pertaining to Frettenham. We hardly need a local newspaper. She never misses a cobweb, talks to herself much of the time (I used to think she was on her mobile), has a good sense of humour, and generally keeps an eye on the property when we are away. Gold dust.

I have lived in my current home for over forty years, and had dental practices in city and county. Cleaners? - I've known a few. The majority have been good decent Norfolk folk. Some have had their quirks, with evaporating sherry, poltergeists moving dresses, and cloned towels, but generally they've been people who I've been pleased to employ, and happy to pass the time of day with. Maybe not Stan. And the vanishing pound coins were really a bonus too far, and required delicate diplomacy in order to maintain valuable family relationships. But this county is my home, I'm a country bor, and Norfolk people are my people. Maybe we're a bit tribal, and therefore feel comfortable together. And so, within reason, we accept one another, warts and all. I love Norfolk people, and I loved my Norfolk char ladies.

# Chapter Six

## Feathers!

*Ostriches, bootiful turkeys, DIY poultry surgery, and the Chicken of the East*

"Watch out. There's a chicken in the road".
Brakes screech. Car horns blast.
"A chicken in the road? There's fifty flipping chickens in the road. Where have *they* all come from?"

The above conversation, or one very similar to it, was probably repeated scores of times, in scores of vehicles, on scores of occasions, between 1999 and 2010. The vehicles involved had reached *Chicken Roundabout.*

\*\*\*\*\*\*\*

Poultry is the term used to refer to domesticated birds, reared for meat, eggs or feathers. The chicken is by far the most common, but the term also includes ducks, geese, turkeys, guinea fowl, squabs (young pigeons) and ostriches.

Ostriches were not an uncommon sight in parts of North Norfolk during the past two or three centuries, though today there are only two remaining. One is at South Creake and the other at Castle Acre. They are pubs, and they have an interesting history.

Sir Edward Coke (pronounced Cook) was born in Mileham in central Norfolk in 1552. He was educated in Norwich and Cambridge, and rose to become Attorney

General under Elizabeth 1, and Lord Chief Justice under James 1. His position and influence brought him great wealth, and he acquired much land, especially in North Norfolk. In 1628, he initiated the saying, 'An Englishman's home is his castle'. He was given a coat of arms with the ostrich as his heraldic symbol. Ostrich feathers were associated with knowledge and understanding. One of his descendants, Thomas Coke, first Earl of Leicester, built Holkham Hall between 1734 and 1738. And so a number of inns within that area adopted the ostrich as their emblem, though only those at Castle Acre and South Creake remain today. Ostriches provide meat and so do the Ostrich Inns (though maybe not ostrich meat), amongst the many dishes on the pubs' menus, alongside a variety of ales. The Inn at Castle Acre is over 400 years old, and both derive their names from the Coke coat of arms. However, when it comes to poultry, it is turkey meat that most people associate with Norfolk.

*******

"Bootiful", said Bernard Matthews – and there were millions who had never heard that word before. He also put Norfolk turkey meat on the map, not to mention on thousands of plates. He was the quintessential Norfolk business man, rising from small beginnings to smile at millions of the television-watching British public, and uttered that one word that will forever be associated with him. *Bootiful*. Norfolk hero, Bernard Matthews, brought the friendly smiling face of the county into innumerable sitting rooms, and with his rich euphonious voice, introduced the nation to the delights of the Norfolk accent. He also sold an amazing amount of turkey meat.

I have outlined something of his story in an earlier volume, mentioning his abortive attempts to rear twenty turkeys whilst a trainee auctioneer. It was a great idea, but he had not budgeted for feeding the chicks, resulting in the project failing. But you cannot keep a good man down, and after completing his two years national service with the Royal Air Force, he became an insurance clerk, but with aspirations. Great Witchingham Hall is an impressive 35-bedroomed, late 16th century building, with Tudor porch, stepped gables and embattled parapets. Insurance clerks don't usually buy such properties, but Bernard Matthews was not your usual insurance clerk. £3,000, and it was a done deal. Maybe it was in a rather dilapidated condition in 1950, but turkeys were not too fussy when it came to such matters. They were hatched in the dining room, reared in the Jacobean bedrooms, and slaughtered in the kitchens, while he and his wife lived in two unheated rooms. They had a 24 hour honeymoon, and worked 13 hours a day, hand-turning eggs and cooking their meals on an upturned gas fire. His vision was to make Norfolk turkey meat affordable for everyone. Hard work and bootiful turkey meat adverts helped make the company a huge success, enabling Bernard to enjoy an amazing lifestyle, complete with Rolls Royce, private jet, super yacht and a home in St. Tropez. He was also an extremely generous philanthropist, supporting countless charities, and giving significant help to projects at Norwich Cathedral, Norwich Hospital, the University of East Anglia, the Princes Trust, the Scout movement and hundreds of other good causes. He especially favoured those in Norfolk. He died in 2010.

Today, Bernard Matthews Foods Ltd employs around 2,000 people, has 56 farms across eastern England, with a turkey turnover somewhere in the region of 7 million

Great Witchingham Hall – turkeys were hatched in the dining room, reared in the Jacobean bedrooms, and slaughtered in the kitchens, while Bernard and his wife lived in two unheated rooms.

birds a year. The company continues to be based in Great Witchingham in Norfolk.

*******

But regardless of the large number of turkeys produced in Norfolk, chickens are farmed and sold in far higher numbers. One company alone, Banham Poultry, based in Attleborough, has an annual turnover of around £100 million, and a weekly turnover of 650,000 chickens.

During my childhood, and throughout my teenage years, chickens were a part of the life of our family. Like many other couples living in rural areas just after the war, and especially whilst rationing was in operation, my parents kept chickens to provide daily eggs and weekly meat. Later, in the months preceding going to University, I spent time working on a farm, cleaning out broiler houses. (A broiler is a hen reared for meat). And when I first moved into the house where I have now lived for over 40 years, I erected a run, bought a chicken house, and kept a few chickens, mainly for eggs, and partly for company. But before I write more about chickens, let me tell you a short story about a Norfolk chicken. And bear in mind that my tongue is firmly in my cheek.

It was in the days when I drove a jaguar sports car. I had an appointment with some people in the west of the county, and not being in a great hurry, was cruising along at around 45 mph. A chicken appeared in my rear view window. On a rural road, in the county of Norfolk, that might not seem particularly noteworthy, except that the chicken was running, and travelling very fast. I thought that it was catching up with me, and then amazingly, it overtook the car. A chicken! I increased my speed in order to keep up with it, as I wanted to see where it was going, or even if it might roll over, dead from exhaustion. It neither slowed down nor rolled over, and in fact, was pulling away from me. The chicken was still in sight as I hit 60 mph, but suddenly slowed down, swerved left, and vanished through the entrance to a driveway. I too slowed down, and overcome with curiosity, proceeded along the driveway until I came to some farm buildings. I parked, turned off the engine, and got out of the car. As I did so, a door in the main farm building opened, and a chap wearing jeans, cotton shirt and cowboy-style hat stepped out. He smiled, and asked if he could help.

"I'm not sure", I replied. "I have been following the most incredible chicken. It overtook my car about a mile back, running like the clappers, and then turned into your drive and vanished".

"That's moine awlroight", said the farmer. "Oi've had a chap doing some of that selective breeding for me. Clever stuff, and could make me a roight ole forchoon. Oi breed chickens, and Oi specialoise in the chicken drumstick market. Blust, this blook and his team, they come up with an amazing noo varoiety of hen. They hev three legs, soo Oi should increase moi prarfits boi 50%. Looks loike a winner, Oi think, but blust they run. Loike loightning. Goo loike the wind, they do".

I could understand the farmer's excitement, and see the commercial potential. But there seemed to me to be a rather important question about these, presumably, genetically engineered chickens.

"But what do they taste like?" I asked the farmer.

"Noo idea", he replied. "Oi ain't caught one yet!"

*******

And now back to something a little more factual. Chickens have been a big part of Norfolk life for decades, and probably centuries. The chicken is a form of domesticated junglefowl, and originated in south-east Asia. The adult male is called a cock, or rooster, and an immature male a cockerel. The adult female is a hen, and the immature female a pullet. They were not kept for food until the rise of the Greek Empire, from around 400 BC, though they were previously reared for cockfighting.

The chicken is found in most parts of the world, and there are more chickens than any other bird. In 2018, it was estimated that their total number was in the region of 23.7 billion, with 60 billion being slaughtered for consumption annually. They first appeared in Britain around 800 BC.

"Barrie - let's go and see if there are some eggs for us this morning", were words from my mother that would cause me to drop whatever I was doing, and head for the henhouse, full of anticipation. That was over 70 years ago, and yet I can still recall the quiet excitement associated with the smell of recently vacated warm straw. And there were eggs! Two or three gently taken from the straw and handed to my mother, completed that rather special and memorable mission for a pre-school youngster living in a small rural village. We had eggs for breakfast daily, and roast chicken most weekends. They were well fenced in by a wire netting run. However, to find one or more roaming around the garden was not uncommon, and involved further adventures of a chasing nature. And if the wire-netting was at times unsuccessful in keeping chickens in, there were also times when it was unsuccessful at keeping rats out. Mother would scream, and Mr. Scripps, our gardener, would appear and dispatch them with wild stabbing and slashing swings of his spade. Also, there were foxes, and at times word got around that chickens were being taken, and my parents would take special care to ensure the run and henhouse were secure.

In those day, the word fox would be uttered with passion. And not of the loving kind. Foxes were seen as vermin of the worst type. Rats could be chased and disposed of by gardeners with spades, but foxes were a different class.

The first recorded fox hunt took place in Norfolk, although hunting the creatures has taken place worldwide for centuries. In 1534, a farmer set out to catch a troublesome fox, using farm dogs. This later developed into foxhunting, which was seen as a sport, and especially with a decline in the number of deer, and hence deer hunting. The particular species was the red fox, and it was chased by hounds with a keen sense of smell, and a *master of foxhounds* together with his team on horseback and on foot. The fox would usually be caught and killed by the hounds. The exercise was known as sport, and there was a degree of romance as the hunt would assemble with the blowing of horns and baying of hounds, red-jacketed huntsmen mounted on beautifully groomed steeds, and villagers gathering to see them off and cheer them on. For those who disapproved of the sport, there were opposing arguments concerning the elimination of vermin, and the value of the coat of the animal. Foxhunting increased greatly during the 17th, 18th and 19th centuries, and though banned in Germany and many other European countries from 1934, continued in popularity in 20th century Britain. But it became increasingly controversial, and though it's a sweeping generalization, was polarised somewhat between the urban population and the more rural countryfolk, and the politically left and the more traditional right. The Burns Enquiry of 1999 led to the Hunting Act being passed in November 2004, which banned hunting with dogs. However, foxhunting continues in Australia, Canada, France, India and Russia, and anti-hunt bodies in Britain quite frequently complain about the illegal flaunting of the Hunting Act by various hunts, who, when accused, quite often retort that they are following legal, artificially laid trails. Which is all rather different from the days when my parents and many like them wished there were more hunts to bring a degree of protection for their back-garden chicken runs where just 2 or 3 dozen hens supplied struggling families with eggs and meat.

My wife, Wendy, was brought up in rural areas of Kent and Suffolk, where her father was a forester, managing an estate, and with a particular interest in trees. It is amazing how Wendy can identify trees in various parts of the world by simply glancing at their leaves. Whilst touring China, our guide asked if anyone would like to guess the name of a particular tree he pointed to. "Pomegranate", said Wendy immediately, to be greeted by, "Shake me by the hand, lady", from our highly impressed guide. "It's the leaves", she whispered to me. But her childhood years in a relatively isolated farmhouse have endowed her with other skills, and sometimes in the evening, whilst sitting on the patio and drinking chilled white wine, she will lower her voice, and say, "Listen to that fox". And I will try hard to identify the coughing she has heard. They are also said to bark, scream, howl, and squeal. Another sound they make is described as 'gekkering' – but the cough carried on the evening air is the distinctive sound, whereby countryfolk identify them.

I was 8 when our family's move to Wroxham saw us with a larger garden and an array of disused stables and outbuildings. My recollections of living there are happy ones, with innumerable opportunities for adventures in garden, stables, sheds, and bordering woods, all under that Norfolk big blue sky. Chickens too enjoyed our new premises, with space to roam (often amongst forests of nettles), and an abundance of rafters on which to roost. My parents would have sacks of grain on which to feed the hens. I wanted to help, and decided to surprise them with a gift. However, the gift involved secretly borrowing from them first, and having cleared weeds from a small area of vegetable garden allotted to me, I furtively took grain from the chicken food sacks, and planted half a dozen rows of it in my patch. Shoots duly appeared, and were tended with painstaking diligence. The various types of grain eventually developed, and were observed daily with excited anticipation. What a pity that there were woods overlooking our back garden, and what a shame that wood pigeons abounded therein. Fat wood pigeons, thanks to the cultivation of chicken food by a well-meaning lad. But we learn from our mistakes, or fail to at our cost. The following year, the tennis net used by my sister and I on our rear lawn when inspired by Wimbledon, went missing for a couple of weeks, and my parents were presented with a modest quantity of mixed grain, much of it still attached to lengths of stalk. Rural life enjoyed in the immediate post-war years, simple pleasures and a healthy lifestyle.

"Stay away Barrie", warned my mother. "I don't want you watching this". Drama indeed, and I was not going to miss out on the ensuing action. My parents had been concerned about one of the chickens which had become weak and sickly. They would discuss the matter in virtual whispers, which provoked my curiosity. What was it they did not want me to hear? I would stroll down to the chicken stable, and observe the hen, shuffling around, or more likely just resting, and not feeding alongside the rest of the brood. My father returned from work early evening, and following another whispered conversation, he strode out of the house heading for the chickens. As he returned, I recognised the ailing creature held firmly under his arm, and followed him back into the house, where he and my mother took it to the scullery, and told me to stay away. They were too occupied to forcibly eject me from the room, and I drew back into the corner, and observed, as mother opened a drawer and produced a sharp vegetable knife.

Food taken in by a chicken passes from the beak, down the throat and into its crop. The crop stores food, and slowly releases it down into the proventriculus, or stomach. Here it is flooded with digestive juices, before moving on to the gizzard, where it is chewed. The gizzard contains small stones that the chicken has swallowed, and muscular movements in the gizzard wall cause the stones to 'chew up' the food. Humans do not need gizzards as they have teeth to do the job. Our poorly hen was crop bound.

"Hold it tight, Dick", said mother. "Watch out for its claws". Our ailing hen had suddenly become quite lively, and extremely noisy, its loud cackling echoing around the scullery walls. Mother was swift and methodical with the knife, and having opened the crop, crudely pulled the contents out, where they fell to the floor. Largely, it was a huge ball of matted grass that had caused the distress. With some difficulty, she sewed up the wound with a couple of large stitches, and father ran back to the run and released the creature. This was home chicken rearing in 1950s Norfolk, which involved DIY veterinary surgery. Without it, the hen would have died. Happily, she lived and continued to produce eggs. She was not a pet, but a part of the economy. If she ailed again, she would be eaten. Our Wroxham years, with memories I will forever treasure, included a few of a somewhat grisly nature.

Being a little nearer the centre of town after our move to North Walsham, resulted in a significantly smaller garden. The original builder had acquired two plots of land, giving us more than twice the area of garden than other houses along that road. But even with garden alongside in addition to that at the rear of the property, we were now in a more built-up area, and there was less space than at our Wroxham home. My parents had priorities in planning a garden. Firstly, there had to be an asparagus bed, and its location was designated before anything else. And secondly, a henhouse and chicken run. Within the confines of our new property, both were of modest size, and instead of scores of hens, we had four. Their function was to produce eggs rather than meat, and with my father's increased seniority in the bank, we started enjoying beef, lamb and pork at weekends.

During my childhood and teenage years, chickens were always there. Usually in the background, and yet an integral part of our lives. Without them, our garden would have been incomplete. Likewise for so many rural Norfolk families. And although the memories are positive, there is so often in life, an exception to prove the rule. Within the context of chickens, the exception came in the form of broiler houses.

I thought it was a simple fruit farm where I picked soft fruit for cash. However, after working there for a few weeks, I and one or two of my friends were called into the office. The management were pleased with our work, and would like to take us on under an hourly rate for the remainder of the summer. Yes please! There was more job security, though we would have to work regardless of the weather. Being taken onto the payroll, I worked normal hours plus evenings, and found out that the farm involved a lot more than strawberry plants and raspberry canes. Bulbs needed grading, presumably because they too were sold. And then I was told to clean out a broiler house. As mentioned earlier, a broiler is a chicken bred purely for meat, and they are generally slaughtered between four and six weeks of age. There were a number of broiler houses on the farm, and within each lived hundreds of chickens. I guess that the size of each house might have been in the region of twenty feet wide and a hundred feet long. The hens started life as a fertilised egg that hatched at around twenty-one days. Day old chicks would then be taken to the broiler house, grow quickly, and be taken to slaughter at six weeks, after which their house would need to be cleaned out in preparation for the arrival of the next batch. We were given large brooms, and manually pushed the litter into huge mounds. And that included dead hens and an abundance of chicken droppings. The intense stench of ammonia was stifling, and the dust created reduced visibility to a few feet. We never wore masks, and found ourselves itching and scratching more than usual during these shifts. At the end of the day, I would cycle the seven miles home, fill the bath and jump in quickly. After submerging completely, I would surface and peer around to see how many bugs and similar were bathing alongside me. That was back in 1963, and I am sure that conditions, both for chickens and workers, have improved since then.

Within the U.K. there are 800 mega farms, of which 74 are in Norfolk. One facility can hold 125,000 broilers, 82,000 laying hens, and 2,500 pigs. The whole concern could be described as industrial, as much as farming. Chickens are a huge industry in Norfolk. In addition to Banham Poultry, already mentioned, there are many other large companies in the county, producing chicken meat and eggs.

"There's a good crop of pigs in that field", laughs Wendy. "Norfolk pigs and Norfolk electricity are taking over whole farms, it seems". Driving through the county these days, Wendy and I are struck by the number of fields full of pigs, and of others given over to solar panels. But the chickens are housed, and out of sight.

The proposed *Chicken of the East* statue would really have raised the profile of the county in a novel and particularly Norfolk manner. However, plans for erection of the statue were turned down by the local council on the grounds that it would be a health hazard. It might not have been as imposing as the *Angel of the North*, but would have put Ditchingham on the map in a manner that would be normal for Norfolk. And it would have preserved the memory of *Chicken Roundabout.*

Not all chickens in Norfolk have lived on farms or in domestic runs, and for a number of years, up to 300 lived on, and off, a busy roundabout. So which came first - the chicken or the roundabout? The story goes, that decades before the roundabout on the A143 appeared, some chickens on an allotment in Ditchingham escaped, and made their home in the grounds of an old maltings, where they found plenty of grain. (Ditchingham, as mentioned elsewhere in this book, is situated on the border, adjacent to Bungay in Suffolk. I was born in

"Watch out Dad", shouted one of my daughters. "Chicken in the road!" We had arrived at Chicken Roundabout!

Ditchingham). They would sometimes stray onto the roundabout, but their home was where the grain could be found - the maltings. Until the maltings burnt down in 1999. Enter Gordon Knowles, resident of the nearby town of Bungay, and friend of chickens. Gordon became known affectionately as 'the 'Ole Chicken Man'. Gordon fed the chickens, and generally cared for them. At times their numbers decreased dramatically, and there were rumours that they were being stolen by chicken thieves. At other times, their numbers increased dramatically, and it was said that people were dumping unwanted broods there during the hours of darkness. After a dramatic decrease to an estimated 70, the RSPCA were called during 2009, and commented that it was possible that foxes were preying on them, or that they might have been stolen or harmed. Some local residents suspected that rat poison was being used, as feelings were running very high on the issue. Should chickens be allowed to make their home on a roundabout? Was it not a traffic hazard? Might people be injured because of the chickens?

"Watch out Dad", shouted one of my daughters. "Chicken in the road!" Followed by, "No. Lots of chickens in the road", as I drove from our home in North Norfolk to visit my parents, who had moved a few years earlier to Bungay. We always arrived at *Chicken Roundabout* where we turned right onto the A143, and my excited daughters would make sure I was aware of the chickens.

'Feathers fly at the *Chicken Roundabout*' ran a Daily Telegraph headline in September 2000, when a dispute arose between the Norfolk County Council, who planned to move the chickens because of safety considerations, and local protesters. *Chicken Roundabout* was becoming famous.

"Look Dad", said excited daughters, gaining my attention, as a reporter on the BBC TV News, announced that, "*Chicken Roundabout* on the A143 in Ditchingham, Norfolk, is the place where a dispute between Norfolk County Council, and local residents who wish to see the site continue, has become quite heated". Hey, it was on BBC TV!

A 'Chicken Roundabout' board game appeared in 2009, in which players had to collect stray chickens and bring them back to - guess where? - Chicken Roundabout. It was for 2 - 4 players aged 5 years or over, and the estimated time involved was given as 30 minutes. I am not sure that it ever really caught on.

'Feathers Ruffled on Norfolk Roundabout' and similar headlines appeared in both local and national newspapers. And then, in 2010, with the number of chickens on the roundabout having fallen to 6, Gordon Knowles decided that it was time to call it a day. The chickens were given to an animal charity, and Gordon went home to roost, so to speak.

In 2012, a plaque was unveiled, celebrating Gordon Knowles and his work and care for the chickens at the roundabout. Plans for the statue, *Chicken of the East*, followed, but were rejected by Ditchingham Parish Council on the grounds that it would be a safety hazard.

And yet that was not the end of the story of *Chicken Roundabout*. In November 2019 a 'mindless idiot', according to local residents, took an SUV several times round the roundabout, churning up and destroying the turf. Was this an attempt to desecrate a historic site, or just brainless vandalism?

Gordon Knowles died in 2020, but *Chicken Roundabout* remains part of Norfolk history. Some of us still lament the demise of these famous hens, and the denial of permission to erect a statue, the *Chicken of the East*.

# Chapter Seven

## *Fur!*

### *Rodents! et al*

"I don't mind you going out into all the world, but do you have to bring so much of it back into our home?", my mother would say, with the suggestion of a smile, emerging from my bedroom and closing the door behind her. Actually, she must have been very tolerant, because such forays and expeditions into the Norfolk countryside resulted in my bedroom resembling a miniature zoo. The stench must have been dreadful, but if you live in an environment, you get used to such things, or simply don't notice them. If it had not been for rodents, I would never have become a dentist. And my mother was very keen that I *should* become a dentist!

Three rodents, each plentiful in Norfolk, were 'significant others' in my life during my teenage years. I loved them - mice, rats and coypus. Today, there are no coypus in Norfolk. However, recent years have brought into my life innumerable encounters with various rodents - mice, rats, rabbits, and squirrels.

And now for the technical information; rodents are mammals, and are characterised by continuously growing, rootless, upper and lower incisors. They are also the largest group of mammals. There are around 5,400 known species of mammal, and nearly half of them are rodents. In the U.K. the largest is the beaver, measuring around a metre from nose to tail, and the smallest is the harvest mouse, weighing less than a 2p coin. One of the most common is the grass-tunnelling field vole, which is also said by some to be the most abundant of all mammals in the U.K. But I have never knowingly seen a grass-tunnelling field vole.

*******

It was something of a shock to my parents when I announced that I wanted to become a dentist. People in our family didn't do things like that. My father was a bank clerk, and his father had worked on the railways. My mother had also been a bank clerk, which was how they had met. Her father ran the family business - haberdashery, drapery and furniture. Her grandfather had managed the company before that, and before him, her great-grandfather; and before that... On that side of the family, everybody was privately educated, and then went into the family business. I was not privately educated, and decided to be a dentist. University? - what was that?

My mother had explained to toddler Barrie that caterpillars changed into butterflies, and when I was still quite young, put some into empty jam jars, added leaves, and demonstrated. It was amazing. I became enthralled with the life that abounded in our Norfolk countryside, would set out with butterfly nets, buckets, etc. and bring back specimens to observe. A frog came to live in a large glass jar beside my bed, alongside further jars containing three species of leech collected from a millpond along lanes a short bike ride from our home. There were larger glass jars with stick insects, purchased from a local pet shop. The stick insects were aliens, but everything else was local. Norfolk. I won't elaborate further - it's in another book.

If you don't look, you don't find. I did not verbalise those words, but mooching along footpaths, I would pause, upturn stones and look under leaves. Crossing a harvested field where straw had been baled, I stopped, considered, and heaved over a bale that was somewhat remote from the stack. Squeak, squeak. Scurry, scurry. Small grey creatures fled and vanished. Mice. They looked cute and cuddly, and I started devising a plan by which I could keep a family of the little darlings in my bedroom.

Looking back to those days, I wonder what type of mice they were. We have five species of native mouse in the U.K., (house mouse, harvest mouse, field mouse, wood mouse, and dormouse), and all but the dormouse are found in Norfolk. Additionally, there is the edible dormouse, introduced to Hertfordshire in 1902 as an escapee. It is rarely found outside that area today. And whereas most mice live for around one year, and the dormouse up to five years, the edible dormouse can attain an age of nine years, if it doesn't get eaten. I have read that the wood mouse is the most abundant of all rodents that live in the U.K. (though, as previously mentioned, there are those that would contend it is the grass-tunnelling field vole). The harvest mouse might seem a prime candidate for hiding under straw bales, and yet I believe my mice were not light brown or honey in colour, but greyish, or dark brown. My guess is that they were field mice, though to the teenaged Norfolk mouser, they were simply mice. And that was around sixty-five years ago.

"Gad! A wabbit", said my mate John. In uttering the word Gad, he was not referring to the seventh son of Jacob, who founded that eponymous tribe of Israel, but was echoing the expression of surprise used by characters in comics and boys' books, back in the 1950s. I always felt it was verging on blasphemy, and avoided it. Rather like 'Gosh' and 'Gee' today. But John lived in the same town as me, went to the same school, and shared my fascination with the Norfolk countryside. We were out on our bicycles, and a rabbit had appeared running down the lane ahead of us. "Wemember my plan", he shouted, pedalling furiously. John's plan for catching rabbits sounded feasible in theory. We were to 'wace along the woad' on our bicycles until we were alongside the fleeing creature, one on either side. Then we would each reach down, grab an ear, and lift it high off the ground. And after that? – well, we would know at the time what to do. In theory, it just about seemed feasible, but in practice, the rabbits would leave the road and bound into the hedge. We never caught a rabbit. Not once. But we did catch mice, and coypus.

John had arrived at our school and entered the second form, which was a year above me. The family had moved to Norfolk. He had a distinctive scar the length of his left arm, which bore witness to an interesting story, of life-saving significance. After becoming a Cub, he graduated into the Boy Scouts at around ten years. Their motto had always been *Be Prepared*. John would need to be. "If you ever cut your wrist, and blood starts spurting out, you have severed an artery. It is then essential that you get a tennis ball and tucked it under your armpit, and bend your arm hard until the bleeding stops. Hold it there, and get to a grown-up as soon as possible. But most people do not carry tennis balls on them, so using one's fist is usually the next best thing".

John had lived in a rural area at that time, and would regularly explore the surrounding countryside, happy with his own company, and that of rabbits ('wabbits' to

John, who had a pwoblem sounding his 'r's), mice, frogs, and many other squeaking, creeping, bounding creatures. Tripping over roots is not uncommon when engaged in such activities, especially when young in years. But tumbling into the shattered remains of a discarded bottle is highly unusual. John was almost immediately aware of warm blood pumping out through his slashed left wrist, and recalling the advice given at Scouts, was prepared. Making his right hand into a fist, he pushed it up hard into his left armpit, brought his left arm across his chest, and ran like a hare until he reached home. A tennis ball was produced, placed into the armpit, and he was rushed to the nearest hospital where he received surgery, was sewn up leaving a long scar, and was told that his prompt action had almost certainly saved his life.

John's ambition, later realised, was to become a vet. His particular fascination was bones. The body of any small mammal found on our wanderings, was popped into a bag, and later placed in a jar of water. "The water wots the flesh off them, and eventually only the bones wemain", he explained. The jars were placed under a hedge in his garden, and one tried to avoid being downwind of it. "You make our garden stink", said his father, but would do anything to help John with his aspiration to be a vet.

John's rather bizarre plan to catch rabbits may have been singularly unsuccessful, but my cunning approach to capturing mice, with which to populate the newly constructed 'mouse house' in my bedroom, yielded several little furry friends. If you, the reader, are inspired to go and do likewise, I can give plenty of advice. Wear old clothes, because you are going to be falling around in recently harvested fields. Wear gloves, or you will find sharp little teeth penetrating the skin on your fingers.

185

That hurts - I found out the hard way. Find a friend, because this is a task that involves teamwork. Wear a jacket with pockets, because you have to transport the little darlings home somehow. And construct a mouse house in which they can relax, exercise, eat, drink, sleep and breed.

In the 1950s and 1960s, school was a place where, amongst other activities, one carried out a certain amount of swapping, buying, selling, and bartering. The currency was usually marbles, cigarette cards, conkers, or other items considered to be of value in the life of young teenagers. Occasionally money. A small snake was a shilling, and white mice, which moved very slowly and were always sniffing, likewise went for a shilling. Rats were a little more expensive, but then weight for weight, you were getting more for your money. Smuggling creatures into school, and later smuggling them out, involved a certain degree of discretion, and a significant amount of darkness, jolting, and disorientation for the animals themselves, usually situated towards the bottom of a satchel or brief case. I needed a decent sized dry aquarium, and one of my friends said his dad had a large glass battery container. (Rechargeable batteries were housed in glass, as they contained sulphuric acid, which reacted with lead to produce electricity). It was over a foot in length, several inches wide, and high enough to prevent the most energetic, acrobatic of mice from leaping out. I was a fret-saw enthusiast in those days, and soon constructed a small house on stilts, with a ramp to the front door. The floor of the container was lined with straw, and the little house placed on it. After that, all I needed were mice.

Perhaps by now you have obtained a large glass container, and constructed your mouse house, and are simply itching to get out to catch mice. You will need a little reconnaissance. You are looking for straw bales, but of a size that are liftable. The more common round bales are far too heavy, but the rectangular stackable bales, more usually found on small farms, are ideal. Having located your suitable hunting ground, find those old clothes, such as you might use in the garden, and gloves thick enough to protect you from bites. John and I would cycle several miles to fields around the village of Felmingham, but today, and if you are adult and a driver, a car is probably your preferred mode of transport. There should be two of you - a puller and a faller. John would be the puller, and would patiently wait, while I would stand and psyche myself up. Mousing should not be unduly hurried. And then a quick nod of the head, or a sharp explosion of "Pull!"

As the bale is pulled away, or quickly flicked over, you fall forwards. But as you do so, you are listening acutely, and at the very hint of a squeak, you change direction in mid-flight. There is a degree of chance, but if at first you don't succeed, try, try again. As the golfer, Gary Player, is reputed to have said, after holing a lengthy putt, " That was lucky, but I have found that the more I practice, the luckier I get". This is a principle that applies not only to golf, but also to selecting shares for investment, extracting teeth, and catching mice under hay bales.

Your aim is to land on a mouse; hence listening for that squeak, and changing direction accordingly. You land with a thump. Is there a wriggle under your tummy? If so, success. If not, it could simply be playing dead, so get up slowly and be prepared to dive again. If there is movement, or a scrambling sensation, or even squeaking, pop your gloved hand under your tummy and gently, but firmly, grab it. Transfer it to your jacket pocket, and zip it up. You are now a successful mouser. It might take a few expeditions, but before too long, you will have enough for a family.

They really need to drink fresh water at least twice a day, and feed on berries, snails, insects, and fungi. I put out cheese for mine (because that was what my father used in his mouse-traps), and they started getting thin. So no cheese, but snails and insects! I kept them for some weeks, in the hope that youngsters would appear, and that my parents and sister would drool over them. But all to no avail. Later examination in the biology laboratory at school revealed that it was a plurality of same-sex relationships. Silly mice - they should have come out from the straw bales two by two, as they did for Noah.

I was a young teenager, easily bored and always into something new. My mouse house was empty, harvest long gone, and the season for hunting small rodents was over. Golden bales under a big blue sky was my idea of mousing weather. Falling onto damp, weed-riddled stubble under overcast cloud was another matter. So off to the pet shop, and once more, my mouse house was occupied. Two trembling (they always trembled - it was their style) white mice, sniffing their way cautiously along my arms and onto my shoulders, were quite a novelty. When they bred, I managed a few sales in the school playground. When they escaped, mother became a degree agitated. And on one occasion, a white mouse vanished, never to be seen again. However, when greyish-white hybrid mice shot out of the skirting boards, raced along the hall, and vanished again, father was irate, mother was dismayed, and my sister and I were quietly amused. I jest not.

The white mice - parents, children, grandchildren and whatever other relations existed in that little house - were eventually transferred into new ownership in the school playground, and rats appeared. White rats. Maybe even slower on their feet than the white mice, not favoured by the rest of the family, and traded in the playground after a very short period of time.

My wife tells me that in the U.K. you are never more than 8 feet from a rat. I will take her word for it. I had first encountered rats in my parents' chicken run at a very early age. Scary. Careering around, running up poles and clearly terrified, whilst chased by our gardener wielding a spade. Again, a story covered in another book. After that, apart from occasionally glimpsing one run across the road, when out driving or walking, I mainly see them swinging on the bird feeders in our garden. 'Squirrel', I thought, the first time I saw one tucking into nuts outside my study window. And then I noticed its tail. Definitely not a squirrel.

However, there were other later encounters with white rats. They were necessary, educational encounters, because I had to know their anatomy. If I was ever to be a dentist. Surprisingly, we never looked at their teeth. Their hearts, kidneys, liver, arteries, and all the other bits that make white rats tick. Except their teeth.

But then the earthworm *lumbricus* had no teeth at all, but we had to study *its* anatomy. Incidentally, *lumbricus* is a genus, and within that genus, there are nearly 700 different species of earthworm. Just imagine - 700 *different* species of earthworm, and all within one genus, *lumbricus*. What sheer delight for a mole, which we will come to a little later. White rats were supplied, I believe, by the education authority. However, *lumbricus*? We dug

189

them up from the Norfolk soil, using a spade. And how did we examine and learn about the parts of these creatures? You really would not want to know. It might make you squirm.

Strangely, the supply of rats dried up. Necessary rats. My friend John had a resourceful and creative answer. Although there was no natural supply of white rats, there was currently, at that time, an abundance, and an infestation, of coypus. I have covered some of our adventures hunting and trapping coypus in a previous book (*Big Blue Sky*, 2022), and am not going to replicate them here. But I will explain that the coypu, also known as the swamp beaver, is related to the capybara, the largest rodent on earth, and a native of South America. Wendy and I have seen capybaras in the wild whilst sailing through the Panama canal. Coypus had escaped from a Norfolk fur farm in the 1930s, and bred to such an extent that the government eventually took steps, and expensive steps at that, to eradicate them. Well, those that were left after John and I had tracked and trapped more than sufficient to study in our biology laboratory.

Today, many people have not heard of the coypu, except when viewing in a zoo. But for several decades, thousands or more of them plagued the Norfolk countryside, eating crops, burrowing under river banks, and scaring little old ladies out of their minds. They also provided me with excitement and adventure, as well as meeting an educational need.

*******

"Just look at my plants", said Wendy. "There's hardly anything left".

It was late spring 2021, and she had been to our small greenhouse to water the recently planted cucumber, courgette and tomato plants. They had been eaten!

And so before planting anything else, we decided to set traps.

"Make sure they are humane traps", said Freya, local friend, spokesperson and protector for every known species of life on earth. "Don't you dare make them suffer".

"Humane?" I retorted. "Have you seen what the little blighters have done to Wendy's plants? Humane? No way. I want the most inhumane trap that man can design. Those mice are going to suffer".

Polite people sometimes call my humour 'ill-judged'. Freya was not so polite, and Wendy thought it would be rather fun to catch them alive and then release them somewhere else. I was informed that the best humane mouse traps were called Mouse Hotels.

Upon Googling mouse hotels, I was directed to a site that informed me that 'MICE stands for Meetings, Incentives, Conferences and Exhibitions. Business tourism at its best. Tailor made hospitality for professionals'. MICE was an acronym, even if I had typed in 'mouse'. Google! But my next hit was spot on.

Hospitality for mice. An acrylic hotel, with red carpet treatment. Well, red plastic up-and-over door treatment, leading to a hallway. The mouse is invited to enter the doorway, trot along the corridor, at the end of which is a mouse banquet. My parents had always tried to trap mice with cheese, but Wendy suggested that peanut butter might be more acceptable. On the choicest wholemeal bread available. And so the banquet was placed at the far end of the hall, craftily, on a small platform, flush with the hall floor, but which would be depressed by the weight of a mouse. Then BANG! Gotcha. The red door would come crashing down, and Mickey or Minnie would await our arrival.

The hotel duly arrived, and peanut butter and luxury bread was placed at the banqueting end, and the contraption was placed in the greenhouse. We retreated indoors, and went to bed. Upon waking the next morning, we were quickly on our way to the greenhouse. Success. A visitor was waiting for us. Maybe he/she had been waiting awhile, but there had been a peanut butter canapé to help pass the time. We gazed at our furry friend. A field mouse. So that was what had been nibbling the plants. We smiled at our cuddly little guest, and I think it smiled back. I then proceeded to take the hotel to a lime pit in some woods a short distance away, and release it. But even with the lovely red door held open, mousey seemed unwilling to pass through it again, and so I tipped it out unceremoniously onto a comfortable tuft of grass. It paused, and then scampered away. Good luck, mousey!

So now Wendy could start planting again, but just for peace of mind, we set the trap once more. The next morning, Wow - another mouse. So there had been two of them.

"No way", said Richard who lives down the lane, countryman with encyclopaedic knowledge of all things Norfolk. "It's the same one. They come back. Paint its toe nails pink, and you'll see. It will be back tomorrow". He paused, and gave his wry grin. "Or cross a river", he added.

And so mousey number two (or mousey number one, returned), still in the hotel, was popped into the Bentley, and transported along Post Office Road, and Hall Lane, before turning right and crossing Penny Beck. (Wendy and I, and our children and grandchildren, love Penny Beck. A short walk of under two miles from our home, a footpath through a wood crosses Penny Beck by a foot bridge. And there, we have all played Pooh Sticks. In fact, so have most of the residents of our village). And then a lay-by, where my furry friend was released and went scampering off into a hay field. Good luck, mousey.

But we set the hotel again, and guess what! So we bought a second mouse hotel, and guess what! So we bought a third mouse hotel, and increased our catch to three a night. I crossed the beck each morning, and as they careered off into the hay field, shouted out, "Have a party".

And then a shrew decided to join in. Two mice and a shrew. Off to the hayfield. But word was getting round. "Go to the hotel. Use the red door. Banquet. Peanut butter and whole meal canapés. Then chauffeured in a Bentley. A rave in a hay field. Don't miss out".

Two more mice, and shrew. More mice. Another shrew. By August, we had caught and released sixty-eight field mice, and three shrews. In one small greenhouse. And yet Wendy provided us with tomatoes, cucumbers, courgettes, and peppers, despite the invasion. And cleaning out the compost bags late summer, she discovered a huge hole under the greenhouse wall. And so it seemed that as fast as we caught them and took them to the hay field, replacements had entered under the wall. Clever little blighters. Shrewed indeed!

"You've had a mischief", said Herbert, an old countryman, with extensive knowledge of rural fauna, flora, and anything else animal, vegetable or mineral that could be found within the county borders. And further afield. "That's what you've had. A mischief". Now, it's many decades since anyone addressed me, and used the word mischief, and he could see that I was totally bemused by what he said.

"A mischief. That's what you had. It's the collective term for mice, and you've had one. Like a murder of crows, or a skulk of foxes, or a blush of robins. But you've had a mischief". So there we have it. Herbert knows these things.

That was new to me. Now I know - when we see several mice together, we are looking at a *mischief*. What an appropriate collective term. A mischief of mice!

And now a little more technical information – shrews are not rodents. They look very similar to mice, but with a longer nose. However, they do not have the rodents' gnawing teeth, but small, sharp pointed teeth. Having been a dentist for many years, I am very much aware of the importance of teeth.

*******

"Mummy, have you got Mrs. Squirrel? Please!", evoked a response of, "Not at home", or, "Yes. Here she is". And if it was the latter response, she would hand me a card, and I would have to say, "Thank you". *Happy Families* was an entertaining, fun and family-bonding card game for winter evenings, especially before the advent of television. And should I forget to say 'Please' or 'Thank

"A mischief. That's what you had. It's the collective term for mice, and you've had one", said Herbert, an old countryman, with extensive knowledge of rural fauna, flora, and anything else animal, vegetable or mineral that could be found within the county borders.

you', I would have to forfeit a card. And that was another function of the Happy Families card game. Good manners, which were sometimes learnt the hard way.

Our *Happy Family* cards had pictures of animals, drawn as friendly cartoon characters. Mr, Mrs, Master and Miss followed by Fox, Mouse, Shrew, Mole and many others, including Squirrel. The object of the game was to accumulate more complete families than one's opponents. And for me, this was my introduction to mice, foxes and many other common garden animals, including squirrels.

The squirrels on our *Happy Family* cards were red squirrels. Technically, they are Eurasian red squirrels, of which there are currently around 140,000 in the U.K. However, the American grey squirrel was introduced here in the 1870s. It is a more robust creature, with greater resistance to disease, and has largely displaced the native, more delicate, red squirrel. The latter are found in some parts of Wales and Scotland, and the Isle of Wight and Cumbria. They are protected, and a few years ago on our annual winter break in the English Lakes, it was a delight to slow down, as one crossed the road in front of us, and then posed on the grass verge, as we slowly passed by.

Red squirrels used to be common in East Anglia, and especially in Thetford forest in the south-west of the county. However, even there they have been almost totally displaced by the grey species.

It is estimated that there are also around 25,000 black squirrels in the U.K. Again, they are not native, but had escaped from a zoo in the early twentieth century. Wendy and I did once spot a black squirrel, but far from Norfolk.

We were on holiday, observing orangutans in Indonesia, when suddenly, the creature leapt in front of us, from one tree to another, and vanished. It was huge. A giant black squirrel.

I must confess that I have a soft spot for squirrels, regardless of their colour or country of origin. We live in an age of diversity and equality, and red, grey or black, they are welcome in our garden. And if there are blue, green and pink varieties yet to be discovered, there is room for those too. Maybe those games of *Happy Families* sowed the seeds when I was around five years of age. In those days, before television, it was such a popular card game for parents to play with children, and I will always remember those colourful, friendly, cartoon characters depicted on our pack of cards, around 75 years ago now. But I can also remember, a few years later, the wonder of watching a squirrel swinging with great agility on a lump of fat attached to a tree branch, intended for birds coming to our garden. We were living in Wroxham, and our kitchen window looked out across the lawn, and the woods that bordered it. Mother would call me to the window to watch, and it was mesmerising. The Wroxham years of my childhood were magical indeed, with access to the woods through broken slats in the rear fence. My mates and I would enjoy cops and robbers, and cowboys and Indians, running in and out and around the trees, but it was there that I became very much aware of such a variety of birds, and a few other creatures too. Magpies were striking, jays shy but beautiful, tits of many varieties delightful, rooks raucous and intruding, pigeons a pest to my father's gardening, and squirrels a joy. An arboreal paradise indeed.

The North Walsham years saw us living in a more urban location, after which I moved to Whitechapel in London, where the closest we had to wild life was the Kray twins. Then Dorset for another five years, after which I returned to Norfolk. We lived in Norwich, where large signs read, *Welcome to Norwich, A Fine City*. And so it is. But it was not until I moved to the outskirts of the small village of Frettenham in 1983 that I became aware again of the rich and abundant nature of the wildlife that is virtually on our doorstep. Or in our gardens.

"Look! There's a cheeky squirrel eating my strawberries. And they are still green", said Wendy, looking out of our sitting room window, and onto the patio, where a grey squirrel was sitting on the table, holding a green strawberry in its front paws, and chewing it, whilst staring at us through the window!

With regard to diet, squirrels are omnivores and opportunists. Their typical food is nuts and seeds, and the more robust grey squirrels tend to seek out high calorie seeds such as acorns, walnuts, sweet chestnuts and similar. They are intelligent in their behaviour, taking items such as acorns and burying them when there is a surplus, and extracting them from the ground during the months when food is scarce. This also helps the proliferation of oak trees, as many buried acorns (and other nuts and seeds) are not retrieved, but germinate, sprout and grow.

Their intelligence in these matters is also applied in two further ways. Squirrels have been known to hide, watch another squirrel burying nuts, and then steal them. Clever. But others are more clever still, and have been seen to pretend to bury nuts, which act as decoys, and lure the thieves away from their intended trophies.

One feature of our garden is a very mature oak tree. As mentioned in an earlier book, a one-time relation, who was born and bred in Norfolk, questioned this fact with the words, "Thet ain't noo ook tray. Thet's an *acorn* tray". She then proved her point by bringing to my attention the carpet of acorns on the ground under it. Silly me. (A few years ago, a bungalow was built next to the wood opposite. Name? 'Acorn House' - but they are *my* acorns!) And there is now a second sizeable oak (or acorn) tree not too far from the original. Around 37 years ago, I noticed an acorn that had sprouted. I planted it in the hedge, tended it almost daily, removing weeds, and watering it during dry spells. My baby. It is now described as 'hooge' by some of my local friends, has a preservation order on it, and is enjoyed by birds of all varieties - and squirrels.

There are lots of jokes about squirrels, and they usually involve nuts. I will share just one, and spare you the other 50. A wise squirrel once said, 'You are what you eat.' He was nuts!

Their intelligence comes into play again when raiding bird feeders. We have found locks and catches removed or bitten through, and some have even circumvented the protection of squirrel-proof feeders. However, they lose respect when stealing birds' eggs from nests, and occasionally fledglings. They also damage arable land by foraging, steal fruit from orchards, and strip bark from trees. For this reason they are described as pests, and from time to time, we have no squirrels in our garden following a cull by local farmers. At the time of writing, Wendy and I have not seen a squirrel in our garden for a few months, and for the first time in living memory, there are red strawberries in our tubs, and our walnut tree is laden with nuts.

They also die on the roads, and can be horribly squashed. One local squirrel was knocked down by a car, killed, but hardly squashed at all, in the lane outside our house. Following a visit to a taxidermist, he has been smiling down on us from the top of a display cabinet for the last 35 years.

Their home? A drey, which looks like a large bird's nest in the fork of a tree. The twigs employed usually bear leaves. And if you spot several squirrels together, you have seen a *scurry*!

*******

You will probably guess that my awareness of rabbits came about through playing *Happy Families*, at an early age. And then there was Beatrix Potter, and *The Tale of Peter Rabbit*. What adorable creatures. My father said they were lovely indeed, and especially in a casserole.

Rabbits are the cutest of little creatures, and when called bunnies, sound almost cuddly. They abound on the golf course where I play, and I love to see their little white rumps bobbing up and down as they scurry away. But my elderly grandfather stepped into a rabbit hole while playing golf, and broke his ankle. I doubt that ankle was ever quite the same again.

They used to scamper round my garden, and after I had first moved in, they accentuated something of the romantic nature of this little pink cottage in its rural setting. They reminded me of Peter Rabbit, who was a lovable mischief. Then they ate all the vegetables that I had planted, and after that, the lower foliage of a hedge I

"You've had a fluffle", said the aforementioned Herbert. "You might not have known that, and some people say colony. But I say fluffle, and so do a lot of countryfolk".

had put between the vegetable patch and the lawn. The hedge was ruined and the vegetables gone.

"You've had a fluffle", said the aforementioned Herbert. "You might not have known that, and some people say colony. But I say fluffle, and so do a lot of countryfolk. It's the collective term for rabbits, like a rabble of butterflies, or a labour of moles, or a prickle of hedgehogs. You've had a fluffle". So now I knew.

"And did you know that a collection of ravens is an unkindness, or sometimes called a conspiracy?" he added. No, I did not know. I sensed that I was about to learn a lot more collective terms, but made an excuse, and escaped indoors for a cup of tea.

There were no rabbits in the UK before the Normans arrived, but they introduced them for food and for their fur. They escaped from captivity, of course, and bred like… well, rabbits. The females are called does, and produce between 3 and 7 babies a month during the breeding season. In the UK, rabbits are here to stay! However, they have many enemies, including me. Their natural predators include stoats, buzzards, polecats and red foxes. In fact, when there has been a dearth of rabbits, such as during those times when myxomatosis was rife, the fox population decreased due to the shortage of food. And then there was yours truly and my gun, which accounted for 5 rabbits in one evening alone around 35 years ago. I had no idea how to skin, prepare or cook them, and so took them into my dental practice the next morning, and the first 5 patients who said they would like one, left with clean teeth and a rabbit.

There were no rabbits in Australia until the 18th century. In 1770, Captain Thomas Cook 'discovered' Australia.

Following a decision to colonise the continent, the First Fleet set sail in 1787, arriving in Botany Bay the following year. They brought with them convicts, settlers, marines, sailors, and - rabbits. They were introduced for neither food nor fur, but for sport. Hunting. However, they proliferated and spread faster than anywhere else in the world, extending across the continent within 50 years, causing irreversible damage to indigenous flora and fauna.

Rabbits competed with cattle and sheep for grass, with devastating effect. In the 1950s, the *myxoma* virus was introduced to control the rabbit population, which was decimated. The virus spread internationally, and *myxomatosis* became a worldwide disease of rabbits. Gradually, a degree of immunity developed, and today, there are an estimated 150 million rabbits in Australia.

How often do I see rabbits in Norfolk today? Every time I play golf, where a dozen or so of the creatures scatter from the fairway, on almost every hole.

And finally on this subject, a rabbit riddle. What did the bunny say when he put his socks on the wrong feet? He said, 'I've mixer ma toesees'.

The European, or brown hare, looks very similar to the rabbit, but it is larger, and its legs and ears are longer. I am always surprised at their size, and their speed. Hares live a more solitary life than rabbits, and do not burrow. Their whole life is spent above ground. They also tend to have a nomadic existence, always being on the move.

They breed in March, and during this month can exhibit bizarre behavior, including boxing perceived competitors, and leaping high in the air at times. This generally excited behaviour is the basis of the expressions 'hare-brained', and 'as mad as a March hare'. And East Anglia is one of the best regions in which to observe them, especially in Norfolk.

\*\*\*\*\*\*\*

"I'm a mole man", said Tom. "Get 'em first time, every time. Just leave 'em to me. I'll sort 'em out". But Tom had not realised quite what he was taking on!

If a Norfolkman can make a mountain out of a molehill, then the Norfolk moles in my garden have the ability to make a thousand mountains out of a molehill. I exaggerate, but you get the general picture.

I bought my little country cottage, in Norfolk but painted *Suffolk pink*, in 1983. It had been on the market for less than a week, and I was the fourth person to put in an offer. My offer was the lowest, but I had nowhere to sell, and so would not become part of a chain that can hold up property sales for months. "Raise your offer £500 and it's yours", was the response, as far as I recall. But George Wilde was a canny Norfolkman, and he then mixed generosity with a shrewd offer. "I'm not charging for the shallots in the vegetable garden, but I'd like £150 for the heating oil in the tank. I've calculated what's there, and that's a fair price". And if I didn't accept? Would he drain it out and take it with him? "Done", I replied, and we shook hands.

The vegetable garden became too much of a challenge for me. Living by myself, redecorating the cottage, learning to cook (shallots should be peeled, cut lengthwise, and heated in oil with butter for 10 minutes), and planting and defending vegetables was too time consuming. It was war. Rabbits seemed to eat most types of vegetables, pigeons seemed to eat most types of vegetables, deer seemed to eat most types of vegetables, and there was precious little left for me. I tried wire-fencing, netting, brightly coloured windmills stuck in the soil, and tin foil fluttering from canes, but all to no avail. And so the vegetable garden was converted to lawn. Well, I smoothed it over, let anything and everything grow, and then doused the whole area with selective weedkiller.

"Pasture", said my good friend and dental colleague, Jim Peirson, after surveying the somewhat uneven nature of it. "That's not lawn; that's pasture". Since when it's been turfed properly.

And now a different war was being waged. Exit rabbits, pigeons and deer. Enter moles.

Let me tell you a few facts about moles. Its Latin name is *tala europaea*. Firstly, for years, I thought that moles were rodents - but they are not. They are members of the order *Eulipotypla*, and are therefore more closely related to hedgehogs and shrews. Having said that, I also thought that hedgehogs and shrews were rodents.

Moles are found all over the world, so I read in an encyclopaedia. But not in Ireland. And yet Ireland is known as the Emerald Isle because of the abundance of lush grass, under which, no doubt, is an abundance of lush worms. So how have the moles missed this amazing habitat? And, of course, there are no snakes in Ireland.

A mole can dig through an amazing 14 metres of soil in just one hour. That is not its speed along its burrows, but the rate at which it travels through solid earth. Like under my lawn.

They are incredibly designed, as one might guess. A cylindrical body, strong shoulders, and large, shovel-like front paws. They are covered in dense silver-black fur, are virtually blind, and yet have an extremely effective sensory system.

There are between 35 and 40 million moles in the U.K., and even if one assumes that half of them live under my lawn, that is still a huge number residing under other people's lawns, and in fields and road verges. (They tend to avoid coniferous forests, moors and sand dunes).

Moles live, on average, for 2 to 3 years, though I am seriously trying to bring this figure down. They can survive for up to 6 years. The usual cause of death is predators, of which I am one, and several mole men I've employed. One in particular, actually catches moles, whereas for the others, I feel that 'mole man' is simply an aspiration. More on that shortly. Other predators include cats, stoats, weasels, and some predatory birds. Interestingly, when I kept cats, I had surprisingly few moles in the garden.

Male moles are called boars, and females are sows. The collective term for moles is a *labour*. No comment!

Their feeding habits are quite fascinating. They run to and fro along their burrows, taking earthworms, and the larvae of flies, beetles, and other insects. They create larders, which are subterranean, spherical chambers, lined with grass. Because their saliva contains a toxin, paralysed worms can be stored in the larder, where they await later consumption. Such larders have been found to contain over one thousand stored worms. And before eating the worm, the mole pulls it through its teeth in order to cause all soil to be squeezed out of its gut. Clever little blighters, aren't they.

The amazing mole facts continue. The mother makes a chamber in the centre of the labyrinth of tunnels, and lines it with grass, moss and leaves. There she has her young, comprising a litter of between 2 and 7. Thankfully, only once a year, and after 4 weeks gestation. When they are around 5 weeks old, she gives them a nasty surprise, pushing them up through one of her mole holes, and then sealing the opening. They are on their own now, and have to quickly start their own tunnels, and find their own food.

It is said that they can spread disease, and rabies gets a mention. However, they would need to bite you in order to infect you, and so humans are reasonably safe. A multitude of other diseases can be spread by the huge number of fleas living within that dense furry coat. So don't cuddle a mole.

"You can set your clock by them", said Les Robertson, professional and highly successful mole man. "They work for 4 hours, and rest for 4 hours. So regular, you really can set your clocks by them". Les heads up a family business, and with military precision, following his career in the forces. No messing - this is war. And Les and his team are on the winning side. The team? - Les Robertson, aka Big Friendly Moler, Jack Robertson, aka Apprentice Moler, and Ben Robertson, aka as Mini Moler. More later, on this amazing family of molers.

I bought my little cottage as an insurance policy. It was beautiful, like a dolls house sitting in a secluded garden. As previously mentioned, it was May 1983. Red roses adorned the front of the property, imparting a delicious, light fragrance to the rural air. It looked out onto the Norfolk countryside. But I did not want to live there. I wanted to be at home with my wife and family. However, that was not to be, and in September that year, I thanked the kind family who had welcomed me into their home for over six months, and moved into the delightful little hideaway that has been my home for over 40 years now. I learnt to cook, my children visited often and stayed frequently, I created enclosures for chickens and ducks, and everything was perfect. Until the moles arrived.

I had previously lived in our nearby city of Norwich, and never had a mole. Prior to that, I had lived in a small town in Dorset, in a small house with a small lawn. There were no moles there. But here, in the Norfolk countryside, overnight, a mole hill appeared.

'What a nuisance', I thought. Well, I had heard about mole hills, and seen plenty in fields and on the verge beside roads. So now I had one in the garden. Fascinating. So a mole had paid a visit. Hope he had enjoyed himself. I took a spade and removed the mound of soil. It left a scar, but it would regrass and vanish after a while. Fascinating indeed. Until the next morning there were three.

A little more spade work, and more unsightly scars. Just a touch irritating. I had never had a mole before, and now one had visited 2 nights running. I hoped it would stay away in future.

But they don't. They hang around, and they breed, and they tunnel at 14 metres an hour, and they clear out those tunnels by pushing soil, debris, and lots of stones up onto the grass. And then they bury back down and do it again and again and again. I was busy with my spade each morning, and the lawn was starting to look like a patchwork quilt constructed by a blind man. And it was getting worse.

There was no Google at that time, and no *Wikipaedia*. One asked around, and in doing so, found that moles were a common affliction for countryfolk with lawns.

"Yer need traps, bor", said Herbert, whose ruddy, weather-beaten face and twinkling eyes suggested a lifetime of outdoor rural experience. "Git yerself some mool traps".

The iron monger in our local town had an ample stock, suggesting a fair demand. I wonder why! I purchased three, and studied the device. It was simple, having 2 big metal pincers which one propped apart with a metal ring. Pop it in a mole run, moley obligingly sticks his head in the ring, and SNAP - a big strong spring grabs him. Hard. Very hard indeed. Goodnight moley!

So a mole hill was removed, and I dug down to find the run. But where was the run? There was no clear run. Maybe pushing the spade into the ground squashed it. Perhaps soil fell into the burrow behind the mole. And so it was largely guesswork. And moley did not obligingly stick his head in the ring. Not just once in any of the three traps. And a week later, fortnight later, month later, I still had not caught even one mole. And the hills kept appearing. This called for deep thought and creativity.

Maybe water was the answer. Had I read somewhere that moles are sometimes washed out of their network of tunnels by flooding after heavy rain. Well, I'd give moley heavy rain! The garden hose was attached to the outside tap, and the squirty end inserted into the mole hole. Whoosh - that should sort the blighter out. Drown, or come belting out of one of the mole hills. I was waiting, spade in hand. Whoosh indeed, as water came spraying *out* of the hole, where it should have been spraying in. Wet trousers from the knees down, and mud covered shoes. I pushed the hose down further, and received a repeat performance. I tried using one of the numerous other mole holes. Whoosh back at me. And so I returned to the drawing board.

I went back to the iron monger, and expressed disappointment. "Yeah, there's a knack to it", he said in a consolatory manner. "There's not many folk actually catch 'em with the traps, but some do. Maybe you need lots of practice. Perhaps you should try smoke bombs. I can order some for you?" Yes he could. I was becoming a desperate man.

The principle was clear, and sounded good. Not so much, 'light blue paper and run', but 'light blue paper, stuff down hole, smokey end first'. Easy. So, I cleared away the hill of stones and soil, and started looking for a clear hole under it. Not always easy, but by the third hill cleared, I thought I had probably found it. Light blue paper. Gentle breeze blows match out before reaching blue paper. Learn from mistakes. Turn ones back to breeze, and light blue paper. Smoke billows up into my face, and I retreat to watch a column of smoke being blown across the lawn by a gentle breeze. But maybe it choked the mole to death, I thought optimistically. The next morning, three more hills. The remainder of my smoke bombs were used in similar manner, and with similar results. And back at the iron mongers, "Yeah, there's a knack to it".

Time passed, and I continued repairing my lawn, but imperfectly, with scarring. "Well, what always works for me…" was a recurring phrase from well-meaning people. But the various methods shared did not necessarily work for others. Or me. And so, my lawn was covered in canes, each with an inverted milk bottle over the top.

"What, yer got moles?" I heard a thousand times. "I never got bottles to work. What you need is little windmills".

And so I covered the lawn with little windmills. It looked rather pretty, except for the scarring, but mole hills continued appearing, and I soon heard someone say,

"What, yer got moles? I never got windmills to work. What you need is to dig them out with a spade. Wait till the top of a newly formed hill starts to twitch, and in yer go. Out with the mole. Bash it. Mole-clear lawn".

I waited. I stood with my spade. Nothing. Boredom. A deck chair on the lawn, and a book to read. Nothing. Give up. Go indoors. Come back out. Fresh mole hill!

"What, yer got moles?" Not always the same person, but virtually the same, rhetorical, question. "Saw yer with yer spade. What yer need is a gun".

Well, I had a gun. Not a shotgun, like so many of the locals, but a powerful .22 air gun. If it had been any more powerful, a fire-arms licence would have been needed. And so I stood. And then I sat. And on those few occasions, when the fresh earth at the top of the hill twitched, CLICK and HISS, and SPUT as a pellet buried itself into the earth. But without success.

"What? Yer got moles? What yer need is a gun".

And yet I did get rid of those moles. The more you practice, the better you get. Traps seemed to be my best chance, and sure enough, the day arrived when I caught a mole. That was not the end of mole hills on my lawn, but after one or two more were trapped with the gadgets, I had a few years of mole-free bliss. And when, a few years later, mole hills started appearing again, I had a cat. And my beautiful Bathsheba was more successful at mole-catching than I had ever been. She would crouch by a partly formed, freshly erupted pile of soil for as long as it took. Pounce! Goodnight moley.

*******

More recently, mole hills had started appearing again. In fact, living in a rural area of Great Britain, this is a problem one will encounter periodically. That is, if you have a garden, and so long as your garden is not part of a sand dune, moor, or coniferous forest. Wendy and I do not have cats these days, as we are away from home quite often. So I reverted to traps, but without success. Maybe the traps were too old and corroded, and so I bought new ones. Around three mole hills were appearing overnight, every night, and a few during daytime. My mole-catching skills of earlier years seemed to have vanished, though I was becoming a dab hand at repairing the lawn. And then Tom arrived, with the welcome words, "I'm a mole man. Get 'em first time, every time. Just leave 'em to me. I'll sort 'em out".

Tom had been to our church. Which is our house, or more accurately, the people who meet in our house Sunday mornings, and some other times. Long story, and not for here. Suffice to say - once an atheist, Damascus road experience, born again, passionate faith, early hours dream, after which we hosted, and continue to host, a church in our home. All covered in other books. Tom had been looking out across our lawn when he had spotted the mole hills. So he was a mole man. I asked him to do whatever was necessary to catch the creature or creatures.

Mid-morning, the next day, I noticed that a car had parked on our drive. At the top of the garden, Tom was busy with a shovel. His wife was sitting in the car, so we invited her in, and called to Tom to join us. Half an hour later, he had still not joined us, and so I ventured out to where he was working. I withheld a gasp. I had thought the moles were destructive, but Tom and his shovel were something else. I held my peace, and a little later Tom joined us, and we drank coffee and put the world to rights. He is a really decent guy, and I always enjoy time with him, listening to his anecdotes of travelling adventures, and of his various hobbies. An hour or two passes quickly with Tom, and as he left, I asked when he would be back. "Tomorrow", he replied. "I always get 'em first time, every time. Just leave 'em to me. I'll sort 'em out".

I sauntered to the top end of the lawn, to find poles and flags where mole hills had been. Turf was carefully replaced. Tom, it appeared, did a lot less damage than moles. But the next morning, there were poles, flags and three mole hills.

"Right", said Tom upon arrival, "Leave 'em to me". As he strode across the lawn carrying shovel, poles, bucket, and flags, we invited his wife in for coffee. They have been friends of ours for a few years, and we enjoy their company. Eventually Tom joined us too, and a little later, on leaving, said, "See yer tomorrow".

The next morning, there were poles, flags and three new mole hills. And during the following three weeks or so, we got to know Tom and his wife better than ever, but we never saw a dead mole. However, we did see many new mole hills. So we stopped talking about moles, and let Tom get on with it. And a month or two later, we realised that we hadn't seen Tom for a few weeks, and I continued to carry out lawn repairs. In fact, for the following few months, *I* started setting the traps again. To no avail.

"I'm a mole man", said Kevin. "Get 'em first time, every time. Just leave 'em to me. I'll sort 'em out". Well, he did not say that *verbatim*, but very much words to that effect.

Kevin had started coming to church-related meetings at our home, and was visibly excited by the evidence of moles. "Would you like me to catch them for you?" I felt I had nothing to lose, and said I would love to see my garden mole-free. "Have you got mole traps I can use, then?" asked my latest mole man. 'Strange', I thought. 'Surely mole men have mole traps'. I told him my four mole traps were in the lawn, and he could pull them out and put them to better use. Around half an hour later, I heard him drive away.

A week or two had passed, and we had not seen Kevin again. The mole traps were still unsprung (meaning that moles were not caught in them), and some little poles he had placed were undisturbed. Not wishing to compromise his mole catching, new mole hills that appeared were left untouched, and although a little like the Pennines, would soon grow to be like the Alps, and then on to the Himalayas. I phoned Kevin on his mobile. "I'll be right round", said Kevin, who I knew to be a busy man, always helping others, always with a heart for the underprivileged. And sure enough, within half an hour, he was busy with a trowel, removing and relocating the traps. After a further two or three weeks of 'waiting for Kevin', I started setting the traps myself again.

"Have you still got moles?" said my friendly, over the road neighbour, Chris. With his wife Joanne, he lives in the aforementioned *Acorn House*. It was more a statement than a question. "My son has been using a professional mole catcher. He's caught two, but the garden is next to a field, and they just keep coming in". And so I turned to our trusty Google, and on typing in 'Norwich' and 'mole catcher', found a short list of professionals. Which is how I came to meet the Team Robertson - Big Friendly, Apprentice and Mini.

"Thirty quid the first one I catch. Twenty quid for each after that. Seven quid fifty pence a visit. OK? And I'll be round every Monday". And so Big Friendly Moler, with Mini Moler at his side, set to work. There were one or two little poles, with fragments of cloth attached, and here and there, metal protruding through the grass. One week later, one dead mole. It was the work of Mini, whose face exhibited more than a little delight. The hills continued appearing, and three weeks later, another dead mole, the work of Big Friendly Moler. And the hills continued appearing, until... mole number three was trapped, after which the lawn lay undisturbed. "I always get the little blighters", said BFM. "If they come back, just phone me, and I'll get 'em".

I feel there's a moral in the mole saga; something to do with not wasting time with hoses and waterbombs and guns and windmills and canes and empty milk bottles, but simply - leave it to the professionals. Not your everyday mole man, but your true professional. He really will 'get the blighters' – (well, he calls them something like 'blighters'!).

# Chapter Eight

## *Attractions!*

*Dinosaurs, stately homes, spectaculars, theatres, zoos…*

"Grandpa, grandpa", shouted one excited granddaughter. "Look. There's dinosaur poos in that field!" And sure enough, at intervals of several yards, we could see huge, dark, glistening clumps of material laying where it had been deposited in a recently harvested field. That was around the year 2008, when 'Becca was about five years of age. But the trail had started for me some thirty years earlier, one morning at my city practice.

"Welcome to my surgery, Mr. Benton. I believe this is your first visit here", I welcomed the pleasant, smiling, gentleman who had just been shown in by my nurse.

"Call me Roy. And it's nice to make your acquaintance", he replied.

That was the first of a number of visits, and I soon came to recognise Roy as a relaxed, modest, well-to-do and thoroughly decent Norfolkman. He lived in the small village of Lenwade a few miles north-west of Norwich, and clearly had many acres of land, of which some were wooded.

"Just drive over sometime", he said with a smile. "There are paths through the woods, and you're welcome to bring your family and explore them". At that time, I had three young daughters, aged from eight down to four years of age, and, a few weeks later, we drove to Lenwade and admired Roy's woods.

"Have you been over?" asked Roy at his next appointment. "Because you need to come again. I've had a surprise placed there!" He gave a broad smile and went on to elaborate. He had commissioned the construction of a life-sized dinosaur (did he say 'in Germany'?) which had been placed in the wood. "Looks like it lives there", he added. "It's fun. I love it".

And it was not too many months after that when Roy, before he laid his head back and opened his mouth, put his hand in his pocket and handed me a wad of tickets. "For you and your family", he said. "My woods have gone commercial. There's quite a few of the creatures there now, and people are coming a fair distance to see them. You'll need tickets, and these should get you in a time or two".

What an amazing place it became, as Roy took those woods back to the Jurassic age, whilst retaining their natural beauty. Meandering paths took one past innumerable life-sized dinosaurs, from pterodactyls in the trees over one's head, to a tyrannosaurus that roared loudly as one passed by, to a brontosaurus that towered high above us. And year by year, the number of dinosaurs grew, and long after Roy had sadly passed on, expanded into café, restaurant, water park and indoor play area. And an 18 hole golf course. And more!

Norfolk may be rather laid back and happily removed from the hustle and bustle of life in some of the country's more urban areas, but we do have a sense of humour. As you leave the dinosaur park, now called *ROARR*, there is

"Looks like it lives there", he added. "It's fun. I love it".

a large sign reading, *WE'RE GLAD YOU CAMEANDSAURUS!*

My little girls enjoyed a quiet family stroll through Roy's woods, and they still do. But now they bring their own children, and we are a sizeable family group, enjoying the U.K.'s largest dinosaur theme park – which just grows and grows.

"We are getting close now", said my wife Wendy, the first time we took granddaughter 'Becca to the park whilst she and her parents were over from their home in New Zealand. "Look! I can see dinosaur poo in that field", pointing to the huge straw bales encased in black polythene. "Poo, poo. Dinosaur poo", echoed Becca excitedly.

At the time of writing, Becca is twenty-one, and I suspect that before too many years have passed, she will point through the window and say to *her* daughter, "Look. Dinosaur poo. We must be getting close now!"

*******

Coco the clown, of international fame, cut the blue ribbon, and the crowd surged forward. One of the inhabitants was Billy, a chimpanzee, who enjoyed smoking a pipe, whilst never refusing cigarettes handed him by passers-by. The year was 1962, the scene was the opening of Cromer Zoo, and there were those who would describe it as *Normal for Norfolk*.

Coco the clown, real name Nicolai Poliakoff OBE, was the father of the proprietor Olga Kerr and her husband Alexander. There were bears, a leopard, an elephant and a host of exotic animals. But with few visitors during the cold Cromer winters, and the high cost of feeding the animals and heating their enclosures, the zoo came under increasing financial pressure.

"Two chickens, a dog and a cat", I said laughingly to my young family when visiting there around the year 1980. "Call this a zoo?" I was exaggerating, but we were rather disappointed by the limited number and variety of exhibits. The zoo closed on Christmas Day 1983. And yet…..

"Wow - this is some improvement on my last visit", I exclaimed around forty years on from my previous time there. Well, it was a different zoo on a different site, and although there was no pipe-smoking chimpanzee to offer cigarettes to (or cats, dogs and chickens), it was Cromer, and there was a variety of interesting creatures from the tropical regions of South America. To be more precise, Brazil, explaining why the enterprise is described in their marketing as Brazilliant. We were visiting *Amazona*.

Ken Sims, who also owns *Thrigby Hall Wildlife Centre* (another highly rated Norfolk 'zoo'), developed 15 acres that was previously a brick works, and populated it with birds, fish and mammals from the Amazon basin. There are big cats, crocodiles, piranhas, monkeys and parrots. Conservation is a strong theme at *Amazona*. And there's a restaurant and play areas, indoor and out, for children, and plenty of green areas where families can picnic, or play ball games.

"Don't get too close", one of my daughters shouted to her young son. He had wandered over to the jaguar enclosure, and Wendy and I agreed with our daughter that the cat had fixed its eyes on the boy with an expression of pure evil. Or perhaps, appetite. The lad was totally safe, with high secure fencing, but I imagined how it must feel to face one in the wild. "Actually, I feel a bit peckish myself", I remarked, and we adjourned to the restaurant for a simple, inexpensive lunch, which rounded off our two hours at the zoo very nicely.

*******

In an age of big screens, small screens, silver screens and canned music of various *genres*, I still feel it's difficult to beat live music and drama. In addition to the entertainment provided, historic and attractive buildings are often the venues. One of the most patronised in Norfolk is the *Theatre Royal* in the centre of Norwich. It is one of the oldest theatres in the country.

Oh yes it is!
Oh no it isn't!
Oh yes it is!

My young grandsons, approaching their teenage years, tried to withhold sniggers, as the characters on stage mending water pipes, suddenly appeared to be peeing huge amounts of water over one another. And then they could contain themselves no longer, and together with the rest of the audience, exploded with uninhibited howls of laughter. It was Christmas. It was the pantomime season, and the theatre was rocking.

But pantomime is seasonal, and for the rest of the year, and for centuries, the Theatre Royal has been entertaining Norfolk people with a huge variety of programmes.

It was in 1730 that a public house called the White Swan, hosted the Comedians. The following year, the name of the establishment was changed to the White Swan Playhouse. In 1757, a theatre was constructed just to the right of the current site, and when it opened in January the following year, the Norwich Comedians became resident there, although the White Swan Playhouse continued for a further 60 years or so. But there was bureaucracy even in those days, and in order to legally continue productions, the name of the building was changed to the Grand Concert Hall. Royal Assent was granted to the theatre a few years later, and since 1768, the name has been the Theatre Royal. The building was totally refurbished twice, until a completely new theatre was constructed on the present site, and opened in 1826.

During its existence, there has been continual remodelling and updating. Oil lights were replaced with gas lights, which in turn were replaced with electric lights. An orchestra pit was constructed. However, in 1934 the building was destroyed by fire, and all productions ceased. Amazingly, the theatre was rapidly rebuilt and reopened the following year.

Today, the *Art Deco* Theatre Royal in Norwich, is one of the country's leading provincial theatres. It seats 1300, and hosts a variety of productions, from touring West End shows, musicals, dramas, opera, ballet, concerts, childrens' shows, to the annual Christmas pantomime. And although Wendy and I are frequently in attendance for a variety of other shows, we always enjoy the panto. As did Josie, our four year old granddaughter, last Christmas. She danced in the aisle, she sang, and she laughed so much. Of course she did. In fact, I think I heard her shout -

"He's behind you!
Oh no he's not!

Oh yes he is!"

*******

For theatre lovers, there is also the *Maddermarket Theatre*, opened in 1921 and housed in an 18th century Grade ll listed building, previously a Roman Catholic church, and the *Norwich Playhouse*, formed in 1995, and which received a Chortle Award for the Best Comedy Venue in the East and Midlands in 2018. The Norfolk and Norwich Festival is the flagship arts festival for Norfolk, runs for around three weeks in May each year, is the largest single city arts festival in the UK, and has its roots back in the 18th century. One should also mention the *Norwich Puppet Theatre*, where I can recall my children being enthralled. That was a few decades ago, but the theatre continues with its fine work. The *Little Theatre* in Sheringham receives rave reviews, as does the *Sewell Barn* in Sprowston. As a boy, my family would often stay in Great Yarmouth or Gorleston-on-sea, and we would go to the *Pavilion Theatre* in the latter. I was too young to understand all the jokes at the summer revue, even though they were only marginally *risqué*, though I can still remember one of them. For those in Kings Lynn, there is the *Corn Exchange*, serving the community with theatre, cinema and Christmas pantomime.

'One of the seven wonders of the British seaside' is just one accolade of the Great Yarmouth *Hippodrome Circus.* It was built in 1903, and has hosted many big names from the world of entertainment. Lily Langtry sang, Houdini escaped, Max Miller joked, and Lloyd George held political rallies there. It is the only surviving permanent circus venue in the British Isles, and one of only three in the world that has a floor that sinks into a pool, for a water show.

My parents loved Great Yarmouth, and we holidayed there often during my childhood years. I would sit in the Hippodrome enraptured, while elephants performed, lions were tamed, and trapeze artists swung high over our heads. A naïve volunteer from the front row was relieved of his wallet, watch and tie by a performing pickpocket, and as the floor sank out of sight, water poured in, and bikini-clad beauties delighted us with synchronised swimming.

"Peter Jay and the Jaywalkers are on at the Wellington pier", said one of my schoolmates. "You know - Peter who was one of the big boys here when we were in the first form?" No, I couldn't remember Peter from my schooldays, if indeed he was one of the big boys at the Paston School. But he was Norfolk, and he did us proud. He had a contract with Decca records, toured the U.K. with the Beatles and Rolling Stones, and took *Can Can 62* into the charts. Now he is owner of the Great Yarmouth Hippodrome Circus, where I continue to be mesmerised by amazing artistes, year after year.

"I daren't watch it Grandpa", said my grandson, looking away from the trapeze artists swinging over our heads. "Me too", I confided, as we held hands and hoped they wouldn't fall on us!

*******

"A chap was upside down, glued to the wall, and about 10 feet off the ground."

"A chap was upside down, glued to the wall, and about 10 feet off the ground".

I sat at the breakfast table in Grandpa and Nana's home in Bungay, captivated by the conversation. Their dining room seemed so large compared to my parents', and people I assumed to be ancestors gazed solemnly down from oil paintings adorning the walls, high above us. Or were they looking at me? My uncle David still lived at home, was a junior partner in the family business, and to my young mind, led a bachelor life of fast cars, glamorous girls, and adventure. The previous evening, he had visited the *Pleasure Beach* at Great Yarmouth, where a new attraction was one of the talking points amongst his set. At 8 years of age, I was totally enraptured.

"It's a large upright cylinder that we enter", he explained. "We have to stand against the outside wall, and once they've closed the door, the wall starts rotating. At the same time, the floor starts dropping. We then find ourselves stuck on the wall because of centrifugal force. The wall spins really fast, and the floor falls away many feet. Well, the chap opposite us was a complete joker, and just as the wall started to accelerate, he flipped upside down, did a handstand against the wall, and stuck to it".

"Did he fall when it slowed down? Was he hurt?" I could just picture the scene, with the fellow hurtling to the floor headfirst.

"Well, he went down with a bit of a bump, and lay on the floor laughing hilariously. But the wall slows down gently as the floor comes back up, and we all landed gently. But most of us landed on our feet, while the man opposite went headfirst of course", he grinned. "And every one of us started stumbling around like we were drunk. It leaves you so dizzy, that you can't walk straight, and several kept falling over. They won't let you out for about 5 minutes. I went on it 5 times".

The Pleasure Beach is situated at the southern end of Great Yarmouth's Golden Mile. One mile of lights, music, crowds, chips, colour and general razzmatazz would appear to draw thousands of largely portly souls, from the Midlands in particular. The Pleasure Beach comprises 13 acres of intensified lights, music, crowds, etc. You might guess that it is not my idea of heaven, and perhaps comes closer to the other place. There are 4 big dippers, where people pay good money to be scared out of their lives, hurtling down from great heights, full throttled, white knuckled, and screaming in terror. I would pay good money *not* to go on them. In fact, there's an abundance of rides, and queues which indicate their popularity. There's a ghost train, which would probably not scare me, and an area for children of all ages. Entry is free. The rides are not. New rides are added. Old ones are removed. Today, I never hear of jokers being stuck upside down, on a revolving wall. Health and Safety rules, and too many banged heads maybe. Times change.

*******

It was a story I had heard from my parents several times. They were probably in their mid-seventies at the time, and I am now older than that. So I understand!

"We came out of the show, and walked back to the car park. Well, it was a huge field, and absolutely full of cars. We realised that we would have to queue for quite a while in order to get out, and so decided to sit in the car and eat our sandwiches before we drove home. Your Cousin Derrick was with us. When we had finished our sandwiches, the car windows were misted up so badly that we couldn't see anything. So we started the engine, put all the blowers on, and started rubbing the windows with dusters. And when we could see out, guess what? We were alone, just us, in the dark, in the middle of this huge field, with all the cars gone, and no-one around. We thought it was so funny".

Yet again, one could say *Normal for Norfolk.* Where else in the world would you come out of a packed variety show late at night, and sit in your car in the dark and eat sandwiches? And find that, having done so, you are alone in the dark in the middle of a huge expanse of Norfolk pasture?

My parents had been to Thursford, a small village in North Norfolk. However, when people say they have 'been to Thursford', they are invariably referring to the Christmas Spectacular, which grew out of a collection of steam engines, which itself started with a Norfolk farm labourer who saved up, and bought a steam roller.

George Thomas Henry Cushing MBE was born in Thursford on 25th March 1904. His father was a farm labourer. George left school at 12, and himself worked as a farmhand, but had a fascination for steam engines. He later worked as a steam roller driver in Kings Lynn, saved money from his wages, bought his own steam roller and began sub-contracting. The business grew, with 15 steam rollers by 1940. Diesel engines rapidly made steam engines redundant, so George bought up unwanted and outdated steam engines, and soon had a fast-growing museum on a farm he had acquired. A tea room and gift shop were added, and the *Thursford Collection* was made into a trust. George died, aged 98, in 2003, and his son John and grandson Charlie are now at the helm. Or wheel.

One item in the collection is the Mighty Wurlitzer, an organ with 1,339 pipes, the fourth largest in Europe, which is central to the famous Thursford Christmas Spectacular. This Christmas extravaganza started in the late 1970s, with a service of carols and Christmas songs performed in a shed, by students from Cambridge University. Today, there is a cast of over 130, and Thursford buzzes. Book early in the year, or you'll not get in. Over 100,000 people descend on the village from all over the country, with scores of coaches transporting them. It is the UK's largest show of its kind, with non-stop music, song, comedy, and other variety acts, all with a Christmas theme.

This is Norfolk. Wendy and I go some years, and parking is still in a huge field. There are cafés and restaurants, and the seating in the auditorium resembled garden furniture when we last attended. Norfolk people are sometimes known as dumplings, and I have to admit that on either side of Wendy and myself, were people who required a seat and a half each, which left us feeling somewhat squashed. *Normal for Norfolk* again maybe. But it is a unique experience, and thanks to the restaurants on site, there is no need to take sandwiches to eat in your car, in the dark, after the show.

Our county abounds with live entertainment; some of it is world-class, and some of it is quite Norfolk. Cromer pier show tends to combine both qualities. Wendy and I visit the end-of-pier theatre around twice a year, and sometimes avail ourselves of the Tides restaurant at the landward end of the pier. "Did you feel the couple of chaps at the next table were... er... rather unusual?" I asked my wife after we had finished our cod and chips and were strolling towards the theatre. "I think you'll see them again soon", she replied. And sure enough we did - they were comedians. Likewise, one can sit and admire the excellent dancing of the glamorous ladies (and their costumes and long, elegant legs) and later realise that, walking back along the pier in the twilight, the three ladies who passed us hunched up in their duffle coats were the self-same girls, going back to their B&B, probably to watch telly for the rest of the evening. These performers are local and they are good, but alongside them are outstanding jugglers and acrobats from around the world.

Cromer pier, voted 'pier of the year' in 2015, is a Grade ll listed building, typically Victorian, and 151 metres in length. However, there are records of a pier being present in 1391, though it was actually a jetty, used largely by fishermen. The theatre is 'at the end', and yet beyond it is the lifeboat house, which itself is amazing and well worth a visit. The theatre is one of only five in the U.K. presenting round-the-year shows, and there is proper theatre seating in both stalls and circle (no garden chairs). The theatre, and its shows, is described as the only one of its kind in the world. It is unique, and it is Norfolk.

*******

What do Anne Boleyn and Tom Jones have in common? The doomed second wife of King Henry Vlll and the Welsh crooner both spent time on the Blickling estate in Norfolk. Blickling Hall is a stately Jacobean building, but was preceded by a Tudor house, the family home of the Boleyns. It is widely believed that Anne Boleyn was born there, around 1501. 500 years later, the Blickling estate is a National Trust property with over 170,000 visitors a year. In addition to exploring a magnificent stately home and beautiful gardens, there is a park with a circular walk around its lake. The estate is just 2 miles from the town where I worked in my county practice for over 20 years.

It's a balmy August evening, and the hillside overlooking the lake hosts a huge crowd of people, of all ages, some with champagne picnics, some in evening wear and others in jeans and T-shirts. There is a buzz of expectation, and all eyes are on the spotlit stage, where the curtains draw back to reveal the celebrity artiste. In 2004, it was Tom Jones, but on other occasions it has been Meat Loaf, or Michael Dublé, or a host of other contemporary musical stars.

Wendy and I are often among the crowd there, and two concerts have been particularly memorable. Together with 2 other couples, we were being entertained by the vocal quartet, *Il Divo*. There were a few drops of rain. And then more, followed by virtual stair-rods descending on us. We were sitting on tarpaulins, and it was time to be resourceful and imaginative. An understatement - we were desperate. Dignity was not a consideration as I crawled under my waterproof sheet, and lay there with my eyes closed, listening to the rain pelting on the exterior. I guess I must have looked rather like an armadillo. Around five minutes later, with the pummeling stair-rods abating, I emerged. My companions? Each was as dry as a bone, and they smiled benignly at me as they folded their umbrellas and tucked them away. The other occasion was the last concert before the pandemic. The array of food and drink caravans lining the perimeter seemed more extensive and attractive than previous years. We indulged. The duck and *Hoisin* sauce wraps were the best we had ever tasted, and I felt compelled to return for replacements, once we had eaten them. All washed down with a bottle of Shiraz.

Alas, I was as ever, the designated driver, but allowed myself just a sip.

The fact that Anne Boleyn was born on the current Blickling estate is the one fact that most local people know of its history, even if historians themselves are uncertain as to the exact year of her birth. She married Henry and became Queen of England in 1533. She was beheaded in the Tower of London on 19th May 1536. She was mother of the future Queen Elizabeth 1. The current building was constructed on the ruins of the old Boleyn residence in 1616. In 1698, the estate passed to Sir John Hobart, the 5th Baronet, who was created Earl of Buckinghamshire in 1746. Hence the Buckinghamshire Arms situated adjacent to the Hall, a 17th century pub and former coaching inn, renowned for its excellent fayre. During the second world war, Blickling Hall was requisitioned as an officer's mess for nearby RAF Oulton. Officers lived in the house, and the servicemen and women were housed in Nissen huts in the grounds. The owner, Philip Kerr, 11th Marquess of Lothian, died in 1940, and the property passed into the hands of the National Trust. The outstanding feature within the Hall is the long gallery, housing the library of 13,000 to 14,000 books and manuscripts.

"Darling", whispered Wendy, "There's a strange man hiding behind one of those stone pillars ahead of us. He's stuck his head out twice, and he was looking straight at you. And he gave me a really funny smile!" I increased the length of my stride, and hastened towards the pillar, and as I got close, "Boo! Got yer - and welcome to Blickling Hall gardens". It was Stephen Hagon, head gardener enjoying one of his less serious moments. He and his wife had been patients of mine for over twenty years, until my retirement, but Stephen was no ordinary patient. He always entered the surgery with a cheeky grin, and warm greeting. He assumed there would be time for conversation (and he was correct) and that I would appreciate his sense of humour when telling me stories and recent anecdotes (which I did). I am sure that Stephen took good humour wherever he went, and it is people like him who make this world a better place. And so Stephen knew that I would appreciate the comedy of the head gardener at this dignified and historic building, jumping out from behind a stone column, and shouting, "Boo!" And now, after 47 years at Blickling, Stephen too has retired, and when he did so, the National Trust recognised the esteem and high regard in which he was held. A garden within the grounds was created as a tribute to him, and he was asked with which shrubs he would like it to be populated. *"Philadelphus"*, he said without hesitation, and I look forward to wandering round Stephen's 'garden' at Blickling in future years, early summer, and enjoying the stunning fragrance of mock orange.

A few years ago we drove a little further into North Norfolk to an open-air concert at Holkham Hall. The main attraction was José Carreras, and to listen to this member of the Three Tenors, with the stunning backdrop of the Hall, was a most memorable experience. No less impressive was an instrumental by the City of London Sinfonia, who were backing Carreras, when they played *Live and Let Die*. Open-air concerts with 'big names' are held there regularly during the summer months, as are many other events. Holkham Hall is an 18th century Neo-Palladian country house. Sir Edward Coke, referred to in an earlier chapter, founded and built up the estate in the 16th century, but it was Thomas Coke, who became the 1st Earl of Leicester, and commissioned the construction of the hall, which took place between 1734 and 1764.

Other stately homes to visit in Norfolk include Sandringham, private country home of the Royal family, Houghton Hall, Felbrigg Hall, Oxburgh Hall, Mannington House and gardens, and Hindringham Hall. I considered myself privileged to have two patients who owned and resided in stately homes within the county, one being a sitting member of the Upper House. The other, a baron, always drove to the practice in a brand new white Bentley Turbo R, whereas his lordship arrived in a small battered, rather nondescript Japanese job.

*******

John Lorien, a beachcomber, was shrimping with his brother-in-law Gary at Holme near Old Hunstanton in early Spring 1998, when he found a bronze ax head. Intrigued, he kept returning and exploring, only to find the roots of an oak tree, upside down in the silt. The Castle Museum in Norwich was informed. This was the second bronze ax head found there. John kept visiting the area, and next discovered that the sea was washing sand away from a circle of 55 oak posts surrounding the central upturned tree roots. The national press published the story, and within three months, five thousand visitors came to view the site. It became known as *Seahenge,* or Holme 1. It was a Bronze Age monument, over four thousand years old, constructed in 2049 BC. Plans were put forward to excavate the site, and move the posts to the Fenland Archeological Trust's field centre at Flag Fen in Cambridgeshire for conservation. This aroused a great controversy locally, where businesses in the area felt it would attract many more tourists, whilst the Norfolk Wildlife Trust were concerned at the disturbance of birds in a nearby sanctuary. And Neopagans and New Age devotees claimed spiritual ownership of the site, and wanted it left untouched.

A probable burial site, it had been built on salt marshes, and was preserved by the accumulation of layers of peat. However, the North Sea is continually causing movement of sands around Norfolk coasts, and this resulted in the site's exposure, and also made it vulnerable to decomposition. Many local people grouped together in an attempt to keep Seahenge on Holme beach, and there was financial backing from the Council of British Druid Orders. But English Heritage was successful in having the posts excavated and removed for preservation in Cambridgeshire, and later in Portsmouth by maritime archaeologists at the Mary Rose Trust. The roots and posts can now be viewed at the nearby *Lynn Museum*.

Shortly after, with relentless tides washing away sand, another ancient circle started coming into view. It was just one hundred metres to the east, and much larger, with two circles of wooden posts. It became known as Holme ll. Archeological investigation found that the two sites had been constructed at the same time. Following the heated debates concerning removal of Holme l, English Heritage decided to leave the second site *in situ*, accepting that, now exposed, it would eventually be destroyed by the sea water.

*******

I produced my arrow, with sharp flint tip. I could kill a buffalo with it. But I would need a bow - and a buffalo. And more than a little practice. We had been taught about Stone Age man (probably Stone Age person in these days of equality. But this was 1954), and how in

I produced my arrow, with sharp flint tip. I could kill a buffalo with it!

Neolithic (New Stone Age) times, he made spears and arrows using flint tips. They were so sharp, and the hunters so skilled, that their weapons would kill buffalo. Likewise in battle, people. I had been inspired. I wanted to make one, and spent time in the woods behind our home, seeking out a suitable length of straight wood. It was springtime, and there was a proliferation of straight, dry basal shoots at the base of a sycamore tree. Well, in those days, it was just 'a tree' to me. And they were simply straight sticks growing out of the bottom of the tree. I cut a few with my ever-present pen knife, and returned home. The best specimen was trimmed to around one foot in length. So far, so good, but finding a flint tip might prove a little more challenging. However, I lived in Norfolk, and there is no better place on earth to find flint.

Flint has been called 'the building block of Norfolk'. There is little natural building stone in the county, but an abundance of flint. It occurs as seams of individual stones of various shapes and sizes, in layers of chalk, and is virtually pure silica. It is as good as indestructible, but will split. Impurities colour the stones, with those from the Fakenham area being brown, whereas black is the hue of those mined around Thetford and Swaffham. If you want grey, then it's North Walsham or Holt. And because of the various factors mentioned, flint is very much a part of the Norfolk landscape, as it has been used in construction for centuries. Flint has been used for building churches, or sometimes just the tower. This is particularly so of Saxon round-towered churches, but it has been extensively used for houses and cottages, and especially so in North Norfolk. Narrow streets and flint cottages greatly enhance the charm of Blakeney on the North Norfolk coast, and many other villages in that area.

However, I did not need to go mining for flint, as there were many in our garden, and especially in the area where the stables stood. Maybe an earlier flint stable or outbuilding had been demolished, or fallen down. I selected two flints, laid one on the ground, and held the other tightly in my right hand. I closed my eyes, and brought my arm down hard. Crack! Crack! Bang! It fractured into two, and the process was repeated. It was potentially dangerous, but my parents did not know, and I was a nine year old boy determined to make an arrow - and it worked. There were large and small shards of flint, and I selected one appropriate for the task. A slit was required in the end of the shaft, and that handy pen knife once again proved indispensable. The theory had been good, but... the wretched flint kept falling out of the shaft. Fortunately, I also made model aeroplanes, and other wooden articles with my fretsaw, and balsa cement was never far away. Three cheers for balsa cement. It took two or three hours to set really hard, and my Stone Age arrow was finished, complete with trimmed chicken feathers glued into slits in the far end as flights. It could kill a buffalo! Maybe.

"I happen to have a Stone Age arrow with me". The other boys and girls in class stared at me, as did Mr. Lowe, our teacher, who had introduced a follow-up lesson on prehistoric England. "Well, I made it, actually", I volunteered, "and I have brought it with me".

"Let's have a look at it", said Mr. Lowe, and I proudly extracted the arrow which was protruding from my satchel. He took it, and examined it carefully.

"I really don't think that Stone Age man used balsa cement, Lawrence!" said Mr. Lowe, and he and the class burst out laughing. But then he smiled and said, "Well done Lawrence. I expect Stone Age man would have used balsa cement if he could have found some. And maybe your arrow is stronger than some of his".

Had I been living in Norfolk four and half thousand years earlier, I might well have gone to *Grimes Graves* to collect my flint. I would have travelled, almost certainly on foot, to just north-west of what is now Thetford. East Anglia had been heavily forested, with Mesolithic man hunting and gathering in the region. But there had been changes, and now in Neolithic times, farming had been introduced by migrants from the Continent. Around, 2650 BC, the same time that Stonehenge was erected, flint mines were constructed in the area now known as Grimes Graves. 433 such mines have been discovered, but a much larger site was actually involved. Each mine was around thirteen metres deep, and the miners descended to the layers of chalk by ladders, where they excavated the jet black flints with deer antlers, before transporting them to the surface. This continued for around three hundred and fifty years, after which tools and weapons were increasingly constructed of bronze. The Bronze Age had arrived.

The flints were used, especially for polished ax heads, and extensively for building dwellings. Centuries later they would be used as strikers for muskets. The mines were largely abandoned and for several millennia, the land existed as sheep pasture. The infilling of the pits left the landscape with a pock-marked appearance. They were excavated in the late 19th century, and today are an English Heritage site. One mine has been fully excavated and is open to the public.

During my first year at the Paston School, we were taught a lot about Grimes Graves, as it was a local site, one of only 10 Neolithic flint mines in the country, and the only one open to the public. But why is the site called Grimes Graves? No, they were not excavated by a man called Grimes, and No, they were not prehistoric graves. The name Grimes Graves, together with Grimshoe Mound, which is situated on the eastern edge of the site, is of Anglo-Saxon origin. The Anglo-Saxons, who dwelt here long after Neolithic man, believed that the landscape was the handiwork of the god Grim (or Woden). The somewhat pitted, lunar appearance of the filled-in mines, led them to believe they were graves. This view was reinforced when a shrine was discovered in one of the pits. Grimshoe is a corruption of Grim's Howe, or Grim's burial mound. Known to the Anglo-Saxons as Grim's Graves, today they are Grimes Graves.

Grimes Graves is an English Heritage site, and also a Site of Special Scientific Interest. It is situated at Lynford, near Thetford, in a nature conservation area, where rare flora and fauna are protected. Although there are well over 400 mine-shafts, only one is excavated and open to the public. You have to be seven or over to go down the ladder and explore the mine, and flat soled-shoes are strongly advised. You will also find the ubiquitous site gift shop. Otherwise, the facilities are rather basic, with portaloos, free parking, and a picnic area. Raw Norfolk!

*******

"How can you spend all your life looking into people's mouths?" asked a lady at a dinner party in the village. In fact, it was more of a statement than a question. And she was not the first to say that, and would not be the last.

"There can be a lot more to dentistry than just staring into mouths", I replied, and went on to explain how I had tried to apply creativity and variety to a career that could have solely involved 'looking into people's mouths'. I was still quite a young dentist when a teacher at a local infants school, where my eldest daughter attended, asked if I would speak to the children about 'Teeth' one morning. I enjoyed that, and so did my daughter, who looked so proud to see Daddy speaking to her schoolmates. After that, I was asked to speak at other schools. A year or two later, I was invited to speak at a Women's Institute meeting. I explained the way teeth developed under the gums, the functions of incisors, canines, premolars and molars, and the chemical composition of various filling materials. I could be so boring! But I happened to mention that the most common way of losing one's false teeth was to vomit them down the toilet, and flush them away before realising that they had gone. Suddenly everybody woke up, and the audience erupted with laughter. So the next time I went to speak at a Women's Institute, I knew what they really wanted - teeth down the toilet, the couple who shared a set of dentures, the night I caught a burglar in the practice, the patient who measured me up for a pair of trousers while I treated his teeth, and so on. And when other groups heard that a dentist was giving a humorous talk and not charging, I was asked to speak at larger and larger groups, involving quite posh lunches and dinners, including those of one of our two main political parties. And there were other aspects of my work that I really enjoyed, and which were far removed from 'staring into mouths'. My Norwich practice was probably the first in the region to publish a six-monthly newsletter, with reader-friendly clinical article, prize crossword, childrens competition, cartoon and so on. Dental practices were not allowed to advertise, but when people heard that we were giving away prizes, there was no need for marketing. I had always enjoyed writing, compiling crosswords - and giving out prizes. And then another opportunity presented, which became a real adventure for me, as well as providing a much needed service for a section of the community. Home visits.

I was asked if I could visit a house-bound patient with arthritis, who needed new false teeth. I was paid a small fee by the NHS for each visit, and although the time involved meant I was carrying out the treatment at a financial loss, it was another break from the surgery routine. Also, since opening my one-surgery practice, patients had flooded in and I had added four further surgeries, three extra dentists, plus hygienists and others. I could afford to help people less fortunate than myself, even if the project lost money. I treated an elderly couple living in a boathouse on the river Wensum, eased dentures with a treadle drill in a remote cottage without electricity, and was accidentally locked in a windowless toilet in Norwich Cathedral Close. With a small portable unit, I carried out cosmetic crown work on a patient in an armchair by the fireside in a tiny Norfolk hamlet, and drank innumerable cups of tea with patients who were basically lonely. I became familiar with towns and villages I would never otherwise have visited, and became adept at route planning. One itinerary took me through Reedham.

Reedham is a village, situated on the north bank of the river Yare, twelve miles downstream from Norwich, and just over seven miles upstream from Great Yarmouth. The village is famous for having one of the last operating railway swing bridges in the country, and for its chain car ferry. The swing bridge was commissioned in the mid-19th century, in order to let wherries through without lowering their large sail. It still opens around 1,300 times a year. But I did not plan my itinerary through Reedham because of the railway swing bridge, but in order to experience the chain ferry. It is the only vehicle ferry in Norfolk. The nearest road crossings of the river are the A47 bridge on the outskirts of Norwich, and the bridge in Great Yarmouth. The ferry can save local people a 30 mile round trip. There has been a ferry at Reedham since the early 17th century, when it was called Norfolk Horse Ferries. Horse-drawn vehicles were ferried across the river, and the chain was hand-wound. This continued until 1950, when it became motorised. I would see two or three patients in their homes in the Reedham area during the morning, and then come to the ferry. The Archer family run both the *Reedham Ferry Inn* and the ferry itself. The inn was always tempting, and then there was the crossing. One would not have to wait too long, and after the two or three cars transported had driven off, I would drive up the ramp and onto the ferry. Sometimes I would be the only vehicle. The ramp would be raised, and the ferry would slowly cross the river Yare. A new ferry boat was built in 1984, and continues to be run by the Archer family. I loved the adventure of crossing the Yare by ferry as part of my day's work, and any visitors to the county might well likewise enjoy this almost unique experience. And, if you have the time and inclination, there is also *Pettitt's Animal Farm* at Reedham, not to mention the *Humpty Dumpty Brewery*, and a two mile stroll along Wherryman's Way will take you to *Polkey's Mill*, a restored 19th century Grade 11 listed wind pump. Reedham can indeed be a great family day out, though for me it was just an adventurous escape from 'staring into mouths'.

## Chapter Nine

## *Big Blue Sky – the seasons*

*A stroll in the snow with Red Legs, blackbirds, bluebells,*
*floods, drought, and deer in the garden.*

*Winter*

Snow! It had been relentless. Big flakes falling out of a grey sky for over 2 days, whilst Norfolk slowly sank under an ever thickening white blanket. The subzero temperatures had lifted a little, and the wind dropped, as I strolled hand-in-hand with Red Legs, under a big blue sky, towards Captain's Pond. We had heard that the ice was super-thick, and a few folk were actually skating on it. The soft crunch of snow under our feet broke the eerie silence around us, as we drew in the crisp, fresh air. There was no traffic. There was no road - just blankets of snow as far as the eye could see, across our Norfolk landscape. Well, snowscape, perhaps.

Captain's Pond, a little over a mile or so from my home in North Walsham, nestled in a hollow, surrounded by woods, the skeletal trees glistening in the cool rays of the winter sun. I strapped on my father's ice-skates, and was soon careering round the pond, my skates hissing across the frozen surface. Red Legs stood with a few other of our friends from the local youth club. Gully was acting the comic as ever, and Stalky's cackles of laughter ricocheted across the glassy surface. I offered to let Red Legs have a turn with the skates, but she giggled and shook her head.

Dusk was approaching, and our little group straggled back towards town. We drifted into twos and threes, and I found myself trudging along with Gully and Hawkeye.

"How long have you and Red Legs been an item?" enquired Gully, with a snigger. Red Legs? Who was he talking about? I was with Pam, who I had met for the first time at the youth club the previous Friday evening.

"Red Legs?" I replied, starting to see where this was going. "I'm with Pam".

"Yeah, Pam. But us lot calls her Red Legs, cos of her legs. Bit like scarlet turnips, specially in this weather". And he laughed again, and dropped back to be with Stalky and Spud.

"He doesn't mean to be a pain. Well, I don't think so", said Stalky. "Red Legs, I mean Pam, has only moved to town recently, and it was Gully that first called her that. Expect she's a nice girl though".

I have always loved the snow. Big flakes. Thickly blanketed fields. It's romantic, exciting, and conjures up images of traditional Christmas cards. It has always aroused the child in me, and has done so for as far back as I can remember. It continues to do so as I approach the end of my eighth decade.

*******

There was a sense of adventure as our ancient, yellow, double-decker school bus skidded and lurched through a veritable blizzard, with visibility down to a matter of feet. The snow was unexpected, and it fell in shedloads, quickly transforming roads and fields into one

The subzero temperatures had lifted a little, and the wind dropped, as I strolled hand-in-hand with Red Legs, under a big blue sky.

continuous covering of pure white. Except we could not see it. Just huge, dancing, white fluffy flakes descending *en masse*, obscuring anything more than a yard or two away.

I guess the school did not want to have around 350 day boys marooned there, and no doubt the bus driver wanted to get home. Local boys slid home on foot, and the other school buses were modern (for 1958) coaches, and left ahead of us. It was a valiant but futile attempt to deliver us safely home. It failed. The bus was overcome by dense and fast growing drifts filling the narrow, winding, wind-swept and blizzard-filled Norfolk country road. I should have been scared. Some of the kids were petrified, and with good reason.

'Wow! What an adventure', I thought, as we were told to proceed on foot. The little girls looked understandably miserable, and so did some of the boys. Not me. I was an adventurer, a polar explorer, and although the seven mile hike, or slide, was quite challenging in places, I arrived safely home with a sense of triumph. There were no mobile phones for us to let our parents know what was happening. It had taken 2 or 3 hours, and I was exhausted, frozen, damp, snow-encrusted - and exhilarated! My parents had gazed through the windows at the blizzard, and probably assumed the school was taking care of us. Or maybe they had phoned the school, and been told we were 'on our way'. My father had returned home from work early, as it was just a mile away. They almost cried with relief when I walked in, though I tried to be self-effacing about my incredible achievement. And looking back, children marching for miles through a blizzard could well have come to serious harm. Exhaustion and hypothermia come to mind. As you might have guessed, there had been no accurate weather forecast to forewarn us, or the school. What an adventure! There was a sequel to the story, resulting in my hero father losing his car and running the risk of being mistaken for the abominable snowman. I share the story in *Big Blue Sky* (2022).

"You love the snow, Barrie. This will help you travel over it", said my father. I was around 8 years old at the time, and stared with excitement at the sledge my father had constructed. I did not know where he obtained the timber, but it weighed a ton. Well, it was certainly heavy. Our home was at the bottom of a *cul de sac*, and the road sloped down to us. But putting the sledge at the top after a fall of snow, resulted in frustration. It just sank into the snow. I tried pulling my sister along on it, and was soon out of breath. It was so *heavy*! I loved my parents, and father put time and energy into looking after the family. Our garden was large enough for me to kick a football around, and so he constructed goal posts for me and my friends to improve our footballing skills. But the sledge was not a success, which was a disappointment. However, years later, with a family of my own, and yet long before the advent of the internet, Google and internet shopping, a mail order advertisement in our national daily caught my eye. And within a week, the sleekest sledge I could ever have imagined was delivered to our home. A smart platform constructed of tastefully stained pinewood, was carried on metal runners, painted bright red. I had to wait a few weeks for snow to fall, and then set out for the hilly, Mousehold heath, with 3 excited children in tow.

"You go first Dad", said eldest daughter Sarah. I gripped the platform, and stooping low, ran along the top of the hill, and reaching the slope down, leapt onto the sleigh. Stomach on the platform, legs straight out behind, and the wind was soon whistling past my ears. A flick of my legs to the left would cause it to change direction. Wouldn't it? Why didn't it? A tree approached, and suddenly Dad lost contact with the sledge. Dad went left, and the sledge went right. Dad was shaken but unhurt. The sledge was dented, but still serviceable. And that sledge continues to be in the family, and enjoyed by those who have the love of snow in their genes.

*******

"Go on Ginger. Do a 'little man' for us", shouted some of the fourth formers, as red-haired Paul, aka Ginger, ran, slipped and skidded his way towards the ice-packed snow slide created in the playground at school. Ginger gained speed, his woolly hat pulled well down and his scarf flying out behind him, and leapt with *panache* onto the glazed, black ice strip. He squatted down, as we all cheered, "Little man", and careered at tremendous speed, almost becoming airborne as he flew off the end and crashed shoulder first into a wall. He stood up grinning, and shaking the snow off, as the next fourth former whizzed along the glistening strip. I was a 'little boy', and together with most other second formers, held fourth form 'big boys' in some esteem. Especially when they did 'little man' on the almost lethal black ice slides. Snow, ice, freezing winter weather - I loved it.

"Go on Dad. Do a 'little man' for *us*". It was 1987, and I realised that I should have kept my mouth shut. My daughters had been enraptured at my stories of snow coming up to the window sills, and of young Barrie enduring a seven mile battle through blizzards and snow drifts of somewhat exaggerated height, when the school bus had become stuck in a drift. I had told them of the thrills of careering along at almost lightning speed, black ice flashing between my feet, as I crouched down and did 'little man' as a fourth former. Now I was 'Dad', and the family was virtually snowed in to our home in rural Norfolk. The side roads were impassable and silent, and my children gazed on with barely-contained excitement as I stamped out the outline of a slide on the sloping lane bordering our garden. A few skids and slides along this area resulted in the packed snow starting to resemble ice, and after around twenty minutes, I was rather stiffly crouching down and zipping along the glassy surface. "Little man", they hollered. When I lost control and found myself rolling along in the snow, there was hilarious laughter, and a flurry of daughters leaping on the slide, and themselves rolling around in the snow. "Little man! Little man", they shouted with excitement. So now there were 5 snow encrusted contenders for the description of abominable snowman.

Today, we have six daughters and twenty grandchildren, living in five different countries. It was late winter 2022, when we had a significant fall of snow. Our New Zealand family continued to enjoy summer, but 3 of our European daughters and families engaged in an igloo competition, whilst Dad looked on and thought, 'I wish......' 'Bricks' were produced from polythene lunch boxes packed full of snow, and used to construct the igloo. A tunnel by which to enter. A main room where the family could eat. Crouched. I felt that my passion and excitement for snow must be genetic, and had been successfully passed on to the groups of widely smiling, excited children and grandchildren, sitting in little white houses in freezing gardens in Amsterdam, Brittany and Norfolk!

Norfolk is the most beautiful of counties when enshrouded in snow. We are on the east of the country, and low lying, with the prevailing winds coming from the south-west. The air rises, passing over the moors of Devon and Cornwall, and the mountains of Wales, Cumbria and Scotland, and having picked up huge amounts of water from the Atlantic, drops it over the high ground. This results in eastern England having less rainfall than the west, and Norfolk being one of the driest counties in the UK - until the wind direction changes. And when the east wind blows in Norfolk, it comes straight from the *Russian Steppes*. And when it is a north-easterly, it comes straight from the arctic. In early March 1947, we had snow up to our windowsills, and in January 1963, *Captain's Pond* froze over, deeply, and I went skating while Red Legs watched and giggled. In both years, the snow was extremely widespread, but I have wonderful memories of Norfolk during the blizzards of 1963. And of Red Legs... I mean, Pam.

"My dogs went out into the snow - and immediately vanished", said my wife Wendy. I have never had a dog. Wendy used to have 15. All at the same time. Tibetan spaniels. She used to breed them, and won a first at Crufts. But 15 - I would never have married her in those days! Snow had been falling, and there must have been two or three feet of it carpeting her back lawn. And the dogs needed to go out. She opened one of the patio doors. Whoosh! All dogs vanished. The snow remained intact, as dogs careered around, creating tunnels. And then they all returned. The snow appeared to be undisturbed.

\*\*\*\*\*\*

One of the prettiest villages in Norfolk, in my opinion, is Ludham. Some of the earliest records of the village go back to 1016, with the founding of nearby St. Benet's Abbey, by King Cnut.

A digression. King Cnut (*Norse*), or Knut, is usually anglicised to Canute. He was king of England (1016), and later of Denmark (1018), and later of Sweden (1028). He was the first of many King Canutes. This first one was also called Canute the Great. He is famous for the story concerning the power of the tide. The truth is shrouded in doubt, and it is probably just a legend. He is reputed to have had his throne taken to the sea shore, where he felt he was so powerful that even the tide would obey him. Which it did not. However, Canute was a godfearing man, and the original account has him commanding the tide to retreat because he wanted to demonstrate that only God has power over the elements.

Now back to Ludham. The church is much larger than one would expect in a village the size of Ludham - but this is Norfolk, and characterised by large churches, due to the prosperity of the wool industry of the 14th century. Later, in the 18th and 19th centuries, Ludham became well known within the region for the design and production of drainage mills. There are many thatched cottages, and I have read that some call it 'the chocolate box village'. Wendy and I have a favourite walk that starts by the church, passes a sign reading 'Crossing' with cast iron ducks along the top of it (to show motorists what might be crossing), and into Lovers Lane. After crossing some fields, we stroll along a narrow lane where there is a vegetable stall. A little further along, the lane joins the main road into the village, and there is another sign. This one is a white board, with hand written large black painted letters. An arrow points in the direction of the lane with the stall, and reads FRESH NORFOLK VEGETABLES. *MUTCH BETTER THAN IN THE*

*SHOPS*. This is Norfolk, of course, and reminds us of another hand-written sign at a junction in a footpath, leading through an animal sanctuary on the edge of our home village, reading *PARTH THIS WAY*. Back to Ludham, and we soon come to the bridge over the river Ant, where one can descend to a footpath along the riverside, and continue for a couple of miles or so to *How Hill*. It is an Edwardian Manor House, and outstandingly attractive. It now serves as a field study station, and outdoor education centre. Some of our local grandchildren have been there on school trips, where they are taken out on the river and broads in an ecologically-sound electric boat, and wander along nature trails, viewing a wealth of natural history. Wendy and I often see herons, lapwings and other waders in the pools and by the riverside. Swallowtail butterflies can be found there in the summer. *Toad Hole Cottage Museum* used to be the home of a marshman, and has been restored to demonstrate their manner of life in the 1880s. And nearby is Turf Fen Drainage Mill, often described as iconic, and appearing on thousands of photographs to portray a typical Norfolk river scene. However, one of our most memorable walks was just after Christmas a few years ago, with the river frozen, a thin blanket of snow carpeting the surrounding fields, the reeds by the river glistening and sparkling in the rays of the low, pale yellow sunlight, and the trees casting long shadows across the meadows. A truly delightful walk at any time of year, but in subzero Norfolk - magical!

*******

2,551 people died, 187,000 farm animals were drowned, and 10,000 buildings destroyed. It was 1953, and it was not just Norfolk that had loss of life and serious property damage and destruction. There was something of a perfect storm, with a deep depression, high northerly winds and a high tide. During the night of 31st January, the northerly winds funnelled waters, already approaching high tide, down the North Sea, where huge waves crashed over the neglected sea defences in vulnerable areas of Scotland, England, north-west Belgium and the Netherlands. By the following day, lives had been lost, and coastal towns and villages were devastated.

I am a Norfolk dumpling, born and bred in the county. My father's work had taken us to Hertfordshire for a few years, where I learnt to toddle, and then to walk, and saw the arrival of a younger sister. But in late spring 1953, we arrived in Wroxham, back in the county of my birth, and moved into a delightful end-terrace house, with afore-mentioned enchanting outbuildings, stables, and woods adjoining our back garden.

At my previous school, there had been a buzz of excitement concerning the impending coronation of Queen Elizabeth ll. At home, I had made a coronation coach from a cardboard kit, and at school, we were each given a coronation mug, with a colourful picture of the Queen with Prince Philip, and the royal coat of arms. I must confess that 2023 brought a degree of nostalgia and a faint sense of *déjà vu*. But before the great day (2nd June) arrived, we had left the village and moved to our new home in Norfolk. And there had been floods.

Floods? At such a young age, I was not exactly addicted to watching the 6 o'clock news every evening. In fact, few people possessed a television in those days, and our source of current affairs was through the radio (called a wireless at that time) and newspapers. My parents were Daily Mail readers, and that paper was an integral part of my childhood. My mother would read me articles that she felt were particularly interesting, or important. One such interesting article also involved a quite remarkable coincidence. In fact, it was the first coincidence that I can remember. My mother had been talking to me about fire engines, which had really caught my imagination. But I had a (please excuse the pun) burning question.

"What happens when a fire engine catches fire, Mummy?" She was not sure that this could ever happen, until a few days later…

"Barrie, just look what I've read in the newspaper. Yesterday, a fire engine was going to a fire, when - guess what? - it caught fire. And so another fire engine was called to help put it out".

More important articles read to me by my mother included Princess Elizabeth and Prince Philip's 1952 visit to *Treetops* viewing lodge in the *Aberdare National Park* in Kenya, where they watched big game at a watering hole. 'Jungles' fascinated me, and continue to do so. Wendy and I stayed at *Treetops* on our honeymoon, and enjoyed the views that Princess Elizabeth and Prince Philip had half a century earlier. But their trip came to an abrupt conclusion when King George Vl died back in the U.K. (in Norfolk), all of which was read to me from the Daily Mail. And in 1953, the devastating floods. My mother had told me to brace myself, even at such a young age, and then shown me page after page of photographs of destroyed and extremely damaged houses, many of which were on the Norfolk coast. A month or two later, we were living in Norfolk, and an enduring memory, and one of my earliest in the county, is the family being taken in my father's Austin 7 along the coast road in the north-east of

Norfolk, quite close to Wroxham, where we were horrified to see the devastation. Some homes had lost entire exterior walls, and every room was exposed to the hostile elements. Norfolk weather had been a powerful force of destruction.

Norfolk is vulnerable to coastal erosion, and was especially vulnerable to such a tempestuous assault. The county's coast was overwhelmed. There were sea defenses, but they were inadequate. Maybe they have been strengthened, but at the time of writing, it is a regular occurrence to read of homes cascading down the cliff face at places such as Happisburgh and Hemsby. If climate change takes the course predicted by some, the sea will invade Norfolk before too many years, and the coastal contour of the county will change dramatically. How many homes will vanish into the North Sea, and how many lives might be lost? Time will tell.

A little further round the coast is an amazing winter spectacle, where you can view around 2,500 seal pups laying on the beach. It is the season when seals breed, and on the beaches of Horsey and next door Winterton-on-sea, the pups can be seen, lying with their mothers, or simply basking in the winter sun.

"There's more water in the car park than there is in the sea", was a slight exaggeration, but the parking area at *Horsey Gap* was rough, with large depressed areas that quickly filled during a rain storm. There are times when we experience rain like stair-rods, but generally, the sun is soon shining again. Horsey Gap was becoming quite popular with sightseers during the seal season, even attracting people from London and further afield. But out of season, it was quiet. I am a practising Christian, with a simple faith involving times of quiet, solitude and prayer.

Horsey Gap ticked all the boxes for me at certain times of year, with innumerable paths through the dunes, and relatively deserted, except for, perhaps, the occasional dog walker. Until news of the seals became more widespread. The car park has now been properly surfaced, and a pay-and-display ticket machine has been installed. More people started coming. Seal wardens roped off areas where dogs might disturb pups, and where parent seals might bite or maul sightseers. Word spread more widely still, and attracted yet more tourists. *Friends of Horsey Seals* supply volunteer wardens to help with traffic and generally see that people stick to the cordoned paths and viewing platforms. And with over 70,000 people visiting between November and January, to view around 2,500 seal pups, an overflow car park is also in use. There are a further 3,000 seal pups born annually at *Blakeney Point*, which are best viewed from the water. Mr. Bean has boat trips daily, weather permitting.

Around 80,000 grey seals, which is half the global population, are to be found around the shores of the British Isles today, whereas 100 years ago they numbered a mere 500. The *Norfolk Wildlife Trust*, of which my wife and I are members, supplies some fascinating facts about grey seals. I quote from their site. *The Latin name for the grey seal, Halichoerus grypus, means hook-nosed sea pig. A colony of breeding seals is called a rookery. A seal's milk is 60% fat. Although the female will mate shortly after the birth of her pup, the fertilised egg does not start to develop until much later. This allows the next pup to be born the same time the following year.*

*Spring*

Springtime, the best time of year, and the season when I can enjoy to the full my two favourite English countryside experiences - the fragrance of hawthorn and the song of the blackbird. Having said that, the blackbird sings all year round. Beautifully, and especially in the spring.

I was so shocked. Kill? That would be worse than criminal. I cannot remember the rest of the rant, but it was part of a conversation of a small group of people after church one morning. The church I went to several years ago. Definitely not the church I'm a part of today. Kill?

She was a lady you wouldn't really want to argue with. Run from, maybe, but not argue with. "Every morning at 5am, a blackbird starts singing outside my bedroom window. It wakes me. I cannot sleep after that. I could *kill* it! I wish someone *would* kill it". I was so shocked. For most of my life, and especially for the 40+ years I have lived in my rural Norfolk cottage, a blackbird has sung outside my bedroom window almost every morning. Well, spring, summer and autumn. Loudly. Melodically. Incredibly beautifully. From very early in the morning during the summer months. And I love it.

The month of May in England is a sheer delight. Our gardens and hedgerows are bursting with new life, colour, vitality, and fragrance, and I am entranced, captivated, and enraptured, year after year, while the blackbird sings almost continuously. I have been particularly blessed with a team of blackbirds, so it seems, serenading me day after day, and year after year. One stations itself outside our bedroom window, perched in a hawthorn tree, whilst its companion proceeds to the top of the garden and takes position in an oak beside the summerhouse. Another would fly to my Aylsham practice, and find a convenient perch outside the surgery window. Seriously, I would have blackbird song to wake me at sunrise, blackbird song to accompany my prayers whilst I spent a devotional time in the summerhouse, and a serenade most of the day from outside my surgery window.

Springtime, and what a wonderful and amazing world in which we live. Recently (spring 2023) we have had great spotted woodpeckers swinging on the nut feeders, *and* hanging on our sitting room window and peering in. Most years, they nest in the woods across the road from us, and male and female visit the bird feeders alternately. Their striking appearance, of pied black and white plumage, with a beautiful red patch on their lower belly, has us spellbound. Males have red on the head as well.

At the time of writing, a sparrowhawk has made its presence known, and is a talking point on our side of the village. It is one of the U.K.'s smaller birds of prey, but still accounts for recent collections of pigeon feathers on our drive. Sadly, their preference is often for song birds, and they soon learn the position of bird feeders. Although they have been seen locally taking wagtails and tits, the populations of these little birds has not noticeably diminished.

Beside us on the patio, a mother blackbird has been feeding her fledgling youngster; blue tits have been doing the same outside my study window, whilst above them, high in the laurel hedge, a pair of pigeons have reared two squabs (young pigeons) in their twiggy nest. One day they stood up in the nest and stretched their wings; the next, they were gone. Squirrels quite often come within a few feet of us in order to drink from our patio water feature.

Planet Earth is truly amazing. I confess that I am a creationist, as I do not have the faith to believe 'it all came from nothing' and 'we've all developed from blobs on the floor of an early ocean'. The beauty and inter-relationships of the *flora* and *fauna* of the countryside, bring about a sense of awe. But as a professional, my knowledge of teeth – their development from soft tissues, and their structure – before ever proceeding to the more complex organs, and physiology and biochemistry of boldily function, leave me in no doubt as to their, and our, origin, whilst respecting the views of those of an evolutionary persuasion. So, don't kill the melodious blackbird - it is part of God's creation, and I praise Him for it, and enjoy it every day.

*******

Norfolk is a rural county, and Wendy and I live on the outskirts of a small village of Viking origin, overlooking a large field, usually of barley, and on another side, woods. On the horizon is a sail-less mill, where local grain used to be ground. The millstones now provide the foundation for the village sign, an attractive wrought iron structure depicting a plough, a Viking longboat, and the mill.

We enjoy the wildlife that inhabits our garden, or simply passes through. However, there is a downside, in that squirrels enjoy green strawberries, even squatting on our patio table whilst devouring them in full sight of us. This year they were unlucky, as the deer got there first. Leaves and stalks would appear to be seen as a nourishing midnight feast to the creatures who visit our garden during the hours of darkness. Likewise, the walnut tree is stripped during springtime, although one recent year saw a dearth of squirrels and an abundance of walnuts. We suspect there had been a cull of the squirrel population, which are deemed to be pests. Needless to say that they are grey. Red are to be adored and protected, apparently, but we love them regardless of colour (politically correct, perhaps), and despite their predilection for green strawberries and green walnuts. And as mentioned elsewhere, last year I caught 68 mice in our greenhouse, plus the odd vole and shrew. The moles can be a nuisance too, and pigeons and pheasants at times devour cherished blooms, or seedlings. We won't mention rats! Last year, starlings decided to make their home under our tiles, and although it was a delight watching them flying in and out with nest-making materials, and later with food for their young, at the end of summer we had to have a builder remove the nest and put the tiles back into place. But this is rural Norfolk, and I would not swap my home here for anywhere else.

Gazing out through the window, strolling round the garden, or walking the local footpaths can lead to serendipitous experiences. Wendy was carrying out a relaxed inspection of the recently acquired hanging baskets and potting plants late spring this year, and stumbled upon (almost stumbled over) a fox, fast asleep behind our summerhouse. But not for long, as it leapt up and shot off through the hedge. And on another occasion, during an evening springtime walk a few years ago, we were graced with the presence of a roe deer (or was it a red, or fallow? It was quite big) emerging from woods beside the lane along which we were walking, and after gazing at us for a minute or so, sauntered off through a

As we approached our village, we were entertained by 3 fox cubs, playing together like puppies, pouncing and rolling, under the watchful eye of their vixen mother.

gap in a hedge. Half an hour later, as we approached our village, we were entertained by 3 fox cubs, playing together like puppies, pouncing and rolling, under the watchful eye of their vixen mother.

We quite often see foxes, and in very differing locations, varying from running across a lane ahead of us whilst rambling not far from our home, to trotting through the local city shopping centre in the small hours of the morning, whilst we are driving to an airport for an early flight. More usually, they are heard rather than seen. Screaming is used to denote and defend their territory from other foxes, and howling and a typical 'yup, yup, yup' call, are associated with mating. But the distinctive coughing is most commonly heard and recognised.

"Stop. I can smell a fox", said Wendy. I was bemused. Was this for real? Again, I was reminded of how her childhood, spent on a relatively isolated country estate, meant that she is aware of sights, sounds and smells that indicate the proximity of creatures of which most of us are totally oblivious. She has found deer tracks on the lawn when damp, and has a field day after snow has fallen.

But it was springtime in Norfolk, and under our typical big blue sky, Wendy could smell a fox. I understand that sniffing the proximity of a fox is a skill that some countryfolk acquire, and employ with great accuracy. I also suspect that this skill is probably even more acutely developed in chickens and other animals that foxes prey on. There were times during my childhood when our chickens would make such a noise during the night, that they were clearly alarmed, and my parents would go running into the garden, and presumably, scare away any marauding fox. I have since read that the smell of a fox is distinctive, musky, and never forgotten. They have a number of glands that secrete scented liquids, but their urine is the main contributor to the odour. "Surely you can smell it too. Stand still. Sniff". So yes - it is musky and distinct, not to be forgotten, and a part of rural Norfolk life.

Springtime, and back at primary school, marbles were jangling in our pockets, or ricocheting off one another in the playground, whilst cigarette cards fluttered down against brick walks, in an attempt to cover one's opponent's card, and win it. Autumn would bring out conkers on lengths of string. You could tell the season by the playground games. But those days are long past for me.

Norfolk is also known as a county that is resplendent with daffodils, which are one of the first flowers to bloom in spring, usually March. They are a sign that winter is over. They have been depicted as a symbol of rebirth. Everywhere appears dead, when suddenly - yellow carpets of daffodils appear.

Blickling Hall is well known for its daffodils. Along the paths of its gardens, there are huge bright yellow carpets, which are said to number in excess of 100,000 of the plants. Tourists and local people flock there, but it is one of just several places where daffodils can be found in abundance in Norfolk. Hindringham Hall, in the north of the county, is a moated, privately owned, medieval manor house, well worth a visit at any time of year. But in March, you will find daffodils by the thousand. And likewise at Felbrigg Hall, another National Trust property, a few miles south-west of Cromer. Since I first got to know Wendy, she has enthused over daffodils, and in March every year, there are scores - or maybe hundreds - alongside our garden paths, and under some of the trees. Even when the flowers have passed, and there are just green stalks and brown petal remnants, I am not allowed to touch them until the leaves have turned yellow. For around 6 weeks after flowering, the plants continue to take nutrients from the soil, and the dead leaves' energy is used in creating the following year's flower.

*******

Does every Norfolk village have its bluebell woods today? We live a few miles north of Norwich, and the bluebell woods on the Blickling estate have been seen as a virtual site of pilgrimage in early May each year. Blue carpets, and the air heavy with their distinctive fragrance, stretching seemingly endlessly through the trees. There are footpaths, and one was almost certain to bump into an old friend one hadn't seen for a few years. And, as a local dentist, I would usually encounter several. "Keep your mouth shut, or he'll be in there!" and similar comments, followed by laughter. But today, driving the 10 or so miles to Blickling, one passes signs inviting people to visit other 'Bluebell Woods'. However, Blickling is outstanding, and in addition to the beautiful blue carpets, one passes the fascinating mausoleum, and also the folly.

Witches thimbles, fairy flowers, and cuckoo boots are some of the names by which bluebells are known. They are a sure sign that spring is in full swing. The bluebell is native to Western Europe, and half of the world's bluebells are found in the British Isles. They grow in ancient woodlands, amongst deciduous trees. They flower before the trees are in leaf, with the sun filtering through the naked branches. When the leaves appear, the sun is largely blocked out, and the blue carpets revert to green woodland floor.

There has been increasing concern at the proliferation of Spanish bluebells. They are described as sturdier, with flowers around their stems, whilst the British or common bluebell has flowers on one side only, of a drooping stem. The Spanish stem is upright. They are a paler shade of blue, and have no scent. The Spanish bluebell is more vigorous than the native species, outcompeting the common bluebell for light and space. It can also hybridise with the local variety, and most urban bluebells today are hybrids.

There are also white bluebells, known as *albino* bluebells, which comprise about 1 in 10,000 of the total number. They are therefore said to be rare, which I did not realise when I bought my present home, and found some in the garden. Having lived here now for over 40 years, I still find both blue and white native, or common, bluebells flowering in our garden every spring. And always under that Norfolk big blue sky.

Another National Trust property, acclaimed for its rhododendrons, is Sheringham Park. There are over 1,000 acres of woodland, gardens and landscaped parkland to explore. And you can take your dog.

Springtime, and the garden becomes alive in so many ways, and not least with birds. They are all so busy, either courting, or establishing and defending territory, and later feeding young. I have mentioned the great spotted woodpeckers, which are one of our favourites.

'A little bit of bread and no cheese'. We were taught that at primary school, and I have never forgotten. We were told that this was the song of the yellowhammer. It really caught my imagination, and I've been listening for it ever since. I'm still listening, but have yet to hear 'A little bit of bread and no cheese' coming out of a nearby bush.

I knew little about birds when I moved into my country cottage (apart from the song of the yellowhammer), but one learns quickly when surrounded by the delightful creatures. 'Tea-cher Tea-cher Tea-cher Tea-cher' dominated my garden, almost to the exclusion of all other sounds. One of my patients, a doctor, was also a birder. A lens for his camera had cost more than his car, and on SAGA cruises, he had a top-rate suite, and dined at the captain's table, all for free. He had to spend a few hours on deck bird-spotting and talking about birds observed and answering questions, and 'I have to wear a white dinner suit in the evenings. More expense', he groaned. But this was serious stuff, and so before numbing him up for a little work on a molar, I tried to describe this invasive bird call. "It's just 2 notes, Kevin. Like a see-saw, see-saw. On and on". And laying there in my dental chair, he made the exact sound. A perfect likeness. "That's it", I cried excitedly. And Kevin explained that it was a male great tit calling for a partner. He also told me that the average Norfolk garden is home to 70 different tits. 70!

So, there were tits other than blue tits? I seemed to recall that my mother had called all small birds swinging on fat balls, 'blue tits'. But Kevin had me thinking outside the box, and these days I identify blue tits, coal tits, great tits, and long-tailed tits in our garden. Almost daily. The tiny long-tailed tits actually look cuddly, and come especially during early morning and early evening, often more than a dozen at a time. They also like to hang on the window frame, seeming to peer in, and tapping away at the glass.

I like to think they are greeting me, and thanking me for the feeders, but I suspect they are really mistaking their reflection for a territorial intruder, and seeing him off. I have not knowingly seen crested tits, but at local RSPB reserves, wardens often point to a twittering emanating from a reed bed, and say, "willow tit" or "marsh tit". So that's two more I've probably seen!

## Summer

'Yippee! The sun's shining, the coast is only 5 miles away, Norfolk is flat, and I'm on school holiday till September. On your bike, Barrie boy'. Maybe I didn't verbalise my feelings in quite those words, but the sun was shining, the sky was blue, and it was early August with several more weeks in which I would feel as free as a bird. I would make some sandwiches, prepare a bottle of orange squash, get on my bike and spend the day enjoying our Norfolk coast.

Living on the southern side of North Walsham, I set off through the town centre, passing the small open market, and the ancient, Newsham fire engine standing in the Market Cross. (In those days, it was of little interest to me that this wooden fire engine dated from around 1725, when it had cost the town £50, was operated by up to 22 men, and had served the community well. In 1974 it was restored by the local fire service, and was not returned to the Market Cross). I pedalled towards Mundesley, pronounced locally as 'Munsly', where my parents had a beach hut. But the wind was against me. And when you're on a bicycle, you discover that Norfolk is not so flat, after all. At least the journey home would be easier, I thought to myself. I arrived at the coastal village of Mundesley, left my bicycle leaning against a fence in the car park, with a security chain hanging through the frame and rear wheel (I believe they are a little more sophisticated these days), and sauntered along the sloping path down the cliffs. A stroll along the beach, sandwiches consumed in my parents beach hut, a swig of orange squash, and back on my bike. Bacton was just south of Mundesley, under 4 miles along the coast road, and once again I realised that Norfolk is far from flat when cycling. Another stroll along the beach, and ready for home, where hopefully, my mother would have prepared one of her excellent stews (my wife calls them casseroles today) with potatoes and 2 veg. Did other meals exist? But whereas my ride to the coast had found me cycling into a head wind, the journey home was no different. Instead of finding the wind behind me and helping me along the way, it had cunningly changed direction by 180°, and was in my face again. I was experiencing the phenomenon of 'land and sea breezes'.

In general terms, in the U.K., the prevailing winds blow in from the south-west. Usually. However, within this overall larger pattern, something different happens along many coastal areas, brought about by the differences in air pressure, which in turn is because the heat capacities of water and dry land are not the same. This proved to be a significant challenge to me during my teenage years of cycling to the coast and back during the summer months.

The sun rises, and radiates heat. The land warms up faster than the sea, causing the air over it to rise, drawing in air from over the sea. This is called a sea breeze. So Barrie boy cycling towards the beach for the day thinks, 'This is hard work, but later today it should blow me home'. No such luck. Later in the day, as the sun sinks in the western sky, the land cools down faster than the sea. Now it is the turn of air over the sea to rise, thus drawing

And when you're on a bicycle, you discover that
Norfolk is not so flat, after all.

in air from the land, and giving the cycling lad another head wind. This is known as a land breeze, or offshore breeze. Norfolk cyclists quickly learn about this phenomenon. Well, this one did!

*******

"Look! Do you see what I see?" said Wendy in a hushed voice. It was late summer 2022, and having been scorched with the abnormally high temperatures, we were now relaxing on the patio with glasses of chilled Chardonnay, in the relative cool of the evening. A large deer materialised out of the descending dusk, and at a leisurely pace, moved across the lawn at the top of our garden. Under the ancient oak that dominates that part of our property, it paused, stared at us in its typically doleful manner, and then slowly sauntered across to the hedge and melted into it. It was a memorable and magical moment.

It was what Wendy and I call 'a proper deer'. It was the type that starts life as a Bambi, and is eventually seen commanding high ground overlooking a Scottish moor, or staring out from a wall in a baronial hall or stately dining room. It was probably a roe deer, as these are the most common in the county. Having said that, I am surprised that the muntjac is not estimated as being the most common, as these are the ones seen most often, not least lying dead beside the road, following a collision with traffic. Indeed, we saw around 5 or 6 dead muntjac on a Norfolk car journey of less than an hour recently, though that number was unusually high. They were introduced from China in the 19th century, and are rapidly increasing in number in the southeast of England, and especially in East Anglia. Similar in size is the shy, and delicate, Chinese water deer. Walking along the bank

A large deer materialised out of the descending dusk, and at a leisurely pace, moved across the lawn at the top of our garden.

of the river Bure near Coltishall a couple of years ago, we disturbed a pair, resting in a wooded area by the water. The sighting was a delight; another serendipitous moment.

All 6 species of British deer can be found in Norfolk. They are roe, red, fallow, sika, muntjac, and Chinese water deer. Roe deer and red deer are native to the county, and fallow deer have been here since the Normans brought them over in the 11th century. It is said that there are currently more deer in the British Isles than at any time since the Tudors, and the evidence on the sides of roads tends to confirm this. The Norfolk red deer is a magnificent creature, and can be 20% larger than those found anywhere else in the country. I have read that the expression 'Monarch of the Glen' should be changed to 'Monarch of the Fen'. Deer are attractive creatures, but in addition to devouring the farmers' crops, and flowers and fruit in our garden, they sometimes cause fatalities on our roads. A patient of mine, successful in business and with a young family, was killed outright when a large deer leapt over a hedge and landed on the Range Rover he was driving. I was shocked that such a lovely family could lose their father in this tragic manner, and yet the number of such fatalities caused by deer is increasing year by year.

Muntjac deer, which are the size of large dogs, and delicate creatures in similar style to the Chinese water deer, also invaders, are rife, and officially designated as vermin. Which they are. Having said that, they are protected by various pieces of legislation, but which did not prevent at least one of them appearing on the menu of an Indian restaurant in the area a few years ago. This is not just a story I heard, but an observation, whilst I scanned through the menu outside the entrance to the restaurant. *Norfolk muntjac vindaloo*. Well goodness, gracious me. Apparently it was not a joke. I took a photograph of the menu. Is this a standard Indian delicacy - or simply normal for Norfolk? Poor deer!

One way of viewing deer in Norfolk, is to visit a deer park. Holkham Hall is situated in North Norfolk, not far from the coast, near Wells-on-sea. The main herd of fallow deer numbers around 500, and many of the bucks have magnificent antlers. Young deer are called fawns until one year old, when they become yearlings. In addition to the fallow deer is a small herd of red deer. At Snettisham Park Farm you can tour the deer park in a tractor and trailer. This is Norfolk! The deer here are red deer, and in their publicity, mention 2 stags and 60 hinds. (In other species of deer, the female may be called a doe, and the male a hart. But with red deer, always stags and hinds). Hand feeding is also part of the deal with the deer safaris at Snettisham. At the Watatunga Wildlife Park near Kings Lynn, one can explore in self-drive buggies or trailer tours, or even stay in one of several cottages that are for hire. There are a wide variety of deer, from many countries, in addition to water buffalo and Barbary sheep.

\*\*\*\*\*\*\*

"Come on Dad. We're getting hungry. Put more paraffin on it".

I never could get the hang of barbecues. The family were young, and the idea of a barbecue in the garden seemed to promise a magical and memorable evening for the family. Those were the days when barbecues were metal bowls on metal legs, with a grilling mesh across the top. One needed a bag of charcoal lumps, and paraffin. And then more paraffin!

"Wait till it gets hot, Dad. Then everything will cook quicker". But sometimes it never got hot. And to add insult to injury, the aromas wafting across the garden fence from other Dads' barbecues always smelt incredibly wonderful.

"Dad, my burger tastes of paraffin". In fact, the sausages tasted of paraffin too. Was that not part of the barbecue experience back in the 1970s?

And then I bought my present home. It was a small country cottage, though it has been seriously enlarged during the last 40 years. It was 1987 and I was starting to have the property modified and extended. Perhaps I could have the brickies build me a proper barbecue. They said they would be only too pleased, and Shawn and Mick duly turned up one Saturday morning, and a few hours later, I was the proud owner of a proper, made-to-measure, custom made, bespoke barbecue. My wallet was much lighter than I had anticipated ("It's the price of bricks these days, mate") but this was the *pukka* article, and would produce *pukka* food.

"Come on Dad. We're getting hungry. Put more paraffin on it". It looked so good, and I had nothing but the best quality tongs, forks, spatulas... There were those rare occasions when, perhaps the wind was in the right direction, or the charcoal was especially flammable, but those occasions were rare indeed. Barbecues were not for me.

And then I noticed other Dads cheating. Gas! And so the builders came back and carried out some demolition work (resulting in a lighter wallet again) and cleared the ground for more productive use. And since that time, I have been a successful Dad and Grandpa at barbecues. Last summer, grandchildren were arriving from France, Amsterdam and also from across the city, half an hour away.

"Grandpa will do a barbecue for when the Amsterdam family arrives, and we'll have a banquet", I emailed and WhatsApped and messaged to our far flung family. The Scottish contingent, and Kiwis were unable to make it, but getting on for a dozen grandchildren, plus parents, around the patio table, with overflow in the dining room, consumed a huge number of eggs, bacon, beans, mushrooms, sausages, and anything else we could find and call 'breakfast food'. Grandson Jonathan had 5 fried eggs, in addition to piles of other fayre, spread out over 3 helpings. And Elisha, Benjy and Caleb were not far behind, and indeed, nor were the granddaughters. It was summertime in Norfolk, and Grandpa is such an expert when it comes to barbecues!

There are a wealth of outdoor activities on offer during the summer months, and some have been memorable. I have mentioned the wildlife trip on Horsey mere ('black-headed gulls have brown heads'), which leaves from the staithe, next to *Horsey Windpump*.

Windpumps are similar to windmills, but they do not 'mill' or grind grain. The wind turns the sails, as in a windmill; the energy is then used to pump fresh water up from a well, or water out of a marsh. Wind pumps are common in Norfolk (I used to think they were wind*mills*) and are used almost exclusively for draining water out of marshland. Horsey Windpump is owned by the National Trust, is open to the public, with 5 floors, 61 steps, and a view across Horsey mere and the marshes. My grandchildren are much braver than me, and together with Wendy, scuttle to the top like lightning. I stay at ground level. I am the official photographer, but at that point, hand my camera to Wendy!

The two of us have also had a nature boat tour around Hickling broad. It was a gift from my daughters for Father's Day. The boat would take 12 people around the broad, and return to the *Pleasure Boat Inn* for supper. In fact, only Wendy and I booked for the trip, which gave us a lot of time to ask questions. At the conclusion, we invited the warden to join us for supper at the inn, which rounded off a beautiful evening.

*******

But our most memorable Norfolk summer, and also U.K. summer, was 1976. It was the hottest, driest and sunniest summer for over 350 years. It was one of the longest droughts in U.K. history, with water rationing, schools closing, and reports of camels riding through Welsh reservoirs. Norfolk is both the driest, and the sunniest county in the U.K., but 1976 was exceptional, and the heatwave intense. My wife and I had 3 little girls under 7. Our lawn was brown, commons were brown, cricket grounds were brown, Mousehold heath was brown. We bought a cheap inflatable paddling pool for the garden to try and help them stay cool. There were forest fires. We were told to place a brick in our toilet cisterns in order to save water. We did not. It was suggested that you 'share your bath with a friend', again to save water. We did not. However, the highest temperature recorded that summer was 35.9°C on 3rd July, and in Cheltenham, not Norfolk. Since then, we have had temperatures topping 40°C. But 1976 is for me, the most memorable. It was an unusual occurrence, though we are now more used to it. Also, it was a British phenomenon that year, whereas since then, it has had a more global impact. And so for many of us, 1976 was the summer by which all other summers are compared. It was a sizzler!

One of the features of summer in Norfolk, is people. Thousands and thousands, thronging the beaches, cruising the broads, cycling the footpaths, exploring historical Norwich, and indulging in a myriad of other recreational activities.

Great Yarmouth is known to some as the Blackpool of the East. Northern accents, large stomachs, shouting children, ice-creams, chips, Bingo, the amusement park, slot machines, more chips, 2 piers, horse and carriage rides, a circus, a marine aquarium, thousands of caravans on hundreds of sites, souvenir stalls stocked with heaps of brightly coloured plastic articles, greyhound racing, an open air market - and more chips. My parents spoke of the town, known locally as 'Yarmouth', as if it was a foretaste of heaven. We stayed at a guest house, and on various caravan sites. We went to shows and saw vocalists, comedians, and other celebrity acts long since gone. The jokes were clean, in those days. It was part of my summertime Norfolk culture to have chips from a bag ("The fish is too expensive. Enjoy the chips"), to be given 12 pennies to put in the slot machines ("Not all at once. Make them last"), and to gaze woefully at the stately horses and carriages, trotting along with excited, beaming parents and children having the time of their lives ("They are far too expensive for *us*. I really don't know who can afford such prices"). Actually, I loved the experience. It was holiday. It was family. It was adventure. And then my parents pushed the boat out, and for 4 successive years, we stayed at Butlins Holiday Camps. More heaven on earth. But over Easter 1964, my first year at University, I joined a party hiking across the

Lake District, which was then, Cumberland and Westmorland. Now it is Cumbria. There are rumours it will revert. I had never seen such beautiful scenery, as we hiked around 10 miles a day for nearly a fortnight, through rain, mist, sunshine and wind. We walked Striding Edge, summitted Helvellyn, were blown flat on our backs by an extreme gust of wind, and engaged in the *camaraderie* of youth hostel life. Magic. Later I discovered Dovedale, on the Derbyshire Staffordshire border. More magic. Holidays that did not involve beach, Bingo, or razzmatazz. I still love hiking those areas, but the quieter areas of Norfolk enchant me.

Burnham Market contrasts strongly with 'Yarmouth'. Whereas the latter may be known to some as 'the Blackpool of the East', Burnham Market is known locally, and in the *Daily Telegraph*, as 'Chelsea-on-Sea'. It is a merger of 3 small villages - Burnham Sutton, Burnham Ulph, and Burnham Westgate. It has been named by *The Times* as one of the poshest 22 villages in England (and the only one in Norfolk), being given 3 posh stars out of 5, but being beaten by Walberswick in Suffolk, which was awarded 4 posh stars. The village boasts a number of independent, upmarket shops, including fashion, deli and interior design. A significant number of properties are second homes, with the owners visiting (from Chelsea?) in order to enjoy the Brancaster Sailing Club, or walk their Labradors on the epic beaches. The *Hoste Arms* is *the* place to stay, and *the* place to dine. If your children are called Peregrine, Quentin, or Ferdinand, or Emmeline, Jemimah or Ophelia, you will feel frightfully and hugely comfortable in Burnham Market.

Morston, Wells-on-sea, Blakeney, Stiffkey, Weybourne, Cley-next-the-sea, and Winterton are quaint, picturesque coastal villages, that Wendy and I love to visit. Some have very good hotels (the Blakeney Hotel, and Morston Hall, are both expensive, but excellent) and most have pubs and inns with rooms (you cannot beat the White Horse at Brancaster), and guest houses. In Cley, you can stay in the aforementioned windmill. There's more than a few stairs to climb, a limited menu, but a first-rate experience. Even in summertime, these places can hardly be described as heaving, though Wendy and I prefer them out of season.

Summer yachting, cruising, boating, paddle-boarding and other water sports are probably oversubscribed on our Norfolk rivers and broads. But if you have to take school holidays, you will probably come in summertime, or pay a school fine, which I understand some parents simply consider to be a holiday supplement. Having said that, Easter and autumn are pleasant times on our waterways, which are well served by riverside pubs and restaurants. Just pray for good weather.

*Autumn*

My birthday is in September, the month that ushers in autumn. So when I was young, September, and therefore autumn, was an exciting time of year. But now that I am elderly, I tend to view the month in a different light. Autumn is not my favourite season, but it is still a season to be enjoyed. It has a lot going for it, as people say today.

"Aren't those trees beautiful! Red, gold, orange. I love the autumn colours", says Wendy, gazing at woods, hedgerows, and lone standing trees. I have mentioned elsewhere that her father was a forester, and trees have been a part of her life since childhood. Likewise flowers, with undisguised excitement at the first appearance of snowdrops, and real glee at the riot of daffodils lining our garden paths and filling beds prior to the later explosion of fuchsia and other shrubs. But autumn in Norfolk brings a panoramic landscape of kaleidoscopic shades and hues.

"They're the colours of death", I used to reply. But I am a 'cup half full' chap, and there are times when I will pause, gaze in awe, and soak in the sheer beauty of some woodland at this time of year. It is just one of the marvels of nature, though it simply enhances my sense of wonder at the Creator.

The colour of the leaves of deciduous trees is determined by pigments. Leaves appear in the spring, and are green. Later, in the autumn, they change colour, and reds, yellows, oranges, golds and others, appear. Why? The variety and intensity varies from year to year. Why? And then they become detached, fall to the ground, and leave the tree standing naked and skeletal. Why?

The pigments are produced by the leaves, and are part of the process by which the tree feeds, using sunlight. The process is called photosynthesis. There are three main pigments involved, of which chlorophyll is the predominant and best known. It is green. There are also carotenes, which are yellow, and anthocyanins, which are shades of red and pink. In spring and summer, chlorophyll is very much the predominant pigment, and leaves are shades of green.

Cold temperatures destroy chlorophyll, and so autumn nights cause the green to fade to yellow. However, if temperatures stay above freezing, the production of anthocyanins is enhanced, and the leaves take on a red hue. If the weather is dry, sugars are concentrated in the leaves, and they become redder still. Autumn sunlight can intensify the redness of the leaves, by further concentrating sugars, and therefore anthocyanins. A layer of cells joining the leaf stalk to the stem starts to break down in the autumn due to hormonal changes in the tree resulting from the lower temperature. At some point the layer fractures, and the wind blows the leaf away. Whether one believes in natural selection or creation, this is a clever arrangement. A tree without leaves conserves water (which is lost through the leaves), conserves energy at a time when the climate is more challenging, and is less buffeted by winter gales, which pass through the leafless branches.

Norfolk has an abundance of woodland, parks and countryside, and there are myriad walks and paths where one can enjoy vibrant shades of red, gold, yellow and orange. A number of such parks and woods have been mentioned already, and include the Blickling estate, Felbrigg Hall estate, Sandringham estate, in addition to Pretty Corner woods and Sheringham Park, both near Sheringham, Lion's Mouth beauty spot at Aylmerton and the Gooderstone Water Gardens and nature trail.

Wendy and I walk in all seasons, and most walks take us through woodland at some point. This is Norfolk. There are many books of walks on sale in most bookshops. We have particularly enjoyed circular walks set along the route of Weavers Way. They take us through a series of quaint Norfolk villages, besides rivers and the broads, across open fields, and through woodland. The air is fresh in open country, but with that distinctive autumnal musky smell where leaves line the pathways. And the colours can be absolutely vibrant.

Summer beaches packed with humanity, shouting, laughing, screaming, splashing and snoring, are transformed with the arrival of autumn. I am not a beach person these days, but on occasions appreciate solitude. I make no secret of my faith, and find lonely spots conducive to prayer. Driving to the beach at small seaside towns and villages, and then walking north or south for 10 minutes or so, can leave one as the sole occupant of that stretch of sand. There might be the occasional fisherman, but the beaches are wide, and one can spend a morning or afternoon without speaking or being spoken to. Norfolk beaches have much to commend them in autumn, with bracing sea air, and an atmosphere of remoteness.

"Are you here for the birds, or have you come to fish?" asked the attendant at the refurbished Norfolk Wildlife Trust (NWT) car park at Cley. Refurbished? - it had been an area of hard packed soil at the end of a lane, adjacent to the shingle beach, and between a wind shelter and the bird sanctuary. Now there was a booth, with a lady attendant collecting parking fees. I waved my NWT membership card, giving free parking to members, and she smiled. And then the question designed to help people park in the appropriate place according to the purpose of their visit. 'Had I come for the birds (right side of the car park) or for the fishing (left side of the car park)?' "I've come here to pray", I responded with a smile. Her face went blank. She closed her eyes and thought. Or prayed, perhaps. And then with a big smile, directed me, "Then you go to the far end and park on the left". Well done, car park lady!

Two other areas of interest enjoyed by Norfolk people, and that attract visitors to the county in the autumn, are deer parks and bird sanctuaries.

The rutting period is the time when stags match up to one another, marked by roaring, posturing, parallel walking, and locking antlers, in a play to impress females, and attain dominance over other males, prior to mating. Red deer and fallow deer rut in the autumn, from late September through to early November, with the roe deer having gone through this routine earlier in the summer.

Deer parks have been referred to earlier in this chapter, and can also be located on the internet. However, be careful if you are in the vicinity of rutting stags. They are wild animals, are pumped full of testosterone and can be aggressive. Advice offered on the various deer sites includes - don't get closer than 50 yards to them, use binoculars to view, use a telephoto lens to photograph, and be very alert. If a stag charges, he will not change his mind and go away. If you run, he will catch you. If you curl upon the ground, he will prong you. So, either climb a tree, or don't be there in the first place!

Norfolk has a large number of nature reserves. The Norfolk Wildlife Trust (NWT) has 32, and the Royal Society for the Protection of Birds (RSPB) has 8. The NWT was founded in 1926 by Dr. Sydney Long, and Cley Marshes (400 acres) was the first Wildlife Trust nature reserve in the country. Nationally, there are now 47 Wildlife Trusts, with some 2,200 nature reserves. I have been visiting the Cley site for a few decades, and have seen the amazing transformation. With a state of the arts visitor centre, video shows, exhibits, restaurant/café, shop, viewing area, etc. it is easily the best in Norfolk and probably the best in the U.K. There are walks of varying lengths through the marshes, and a variety of hides looking out across the salt marshes and scrapes. (A *scrape* is an artificial pool for, especially, waders. It is created using a digger, to varying depths of less than a metre, typically in a reserve for water birds). There is a well-defined circular walk of around 2 miles, and Cley beach, which forms part of the Norfolk Coastal path. I am not so knowledgeable about birds, but the avocet is unmistakeable, and one can become mesmerised watching godwits, curlews, sandpipers, ducks and geese of every description, pipits, snipes, spoonbills.... whilst marsh harriers glide over the landward area of the marshes, patrolling and hunting frogs, small mammals and birds. One internet site states that at Cley, one can view 'rarities of all shapes and sizes'.

NWT and RSPB reserves can be located through the internet. One hesitates to name some for fear of omitting others of significance. This is Norfolk, and we have so many amazing reserves across the county, by the seashore, on the broads, and inland in woodland.

There is spectacular bird watching at so many reserves in Norfolk, with the autumn migrations attracting huge numbers of birders, armed with camera lenses like bazookas, and binoculars swinging round their necks. Many companies offer package holidays to Norfolk reserves, simply to view the amazing sights during the autumn months. The RSPB reserve at Snettisham describes what they call the Whirling Wader Spectacular, as high autumn tides push tens of thousands of waders into the air, which whirl around in vast murmurations. Cackling flocks of pink-footed geese, numbering tens of thousands, arrive from their breeding grounds in Iceland, overwinter, and depart in the spring. At other times,

50,000 waders take to the air at once, which is both breathtaking and spectacular.

"By the way", said Hugh, with a beguiling smile, "My annual exhibition is on at the White Hart Gallery next week. Just in case you're interested". Hugh Brandon-Cox was an explorer, artist and writer, who had lived in a log cabin in Lapland, written about wildlife in the arctic circle, made films with the BBC and Sir Richard Attenborough ('Dickie' to Hugh), and eventually settled in Norfolk, where he became enamoured by the wind-swept, timeless northern coastline and wildlife. His father, the naturalist and explorer, Colonel John Brandon-Cox, had been killed in a Zulu uprising in 1917, a few months before Hugh was born, and was his lifelong inspiration. Hugh was a patient at my county practice.

"Let's go to Hugh's exhibition darling. I love his work, and I promise not to buy any of his paintings. I mean, ask *you* to buy any. Promise". Even if Hugh forgot to mention his exhibitions to me, he always remembered to tell Dawn, to whom I was married at that time. He was planting a seed, and he knew it. That beguiling smile!

The following week, at the exhibition, I was to hear the words, "I'm so sorry, but I've fallen in love with another of Hugh's paintings. I want it so much. *Please!*" Which resulted in us building up a small collection of Hugh's originals. Just one or two a year, when he exhibited at the *White Hart Gallery.* That was back in the 1980s and 1990s. Hugh passed away in 2004. My wife Dawn had left for Canada, and a new husband (well, at least two so far, I've heard) in 2001, but Hugh's paintings continue to adorn my sitting room and bedroom walls. He painted the Norfolk countryside, but only in an autumn or winter setting. I also have his rendering of a pheasant, another of a badger, and a third of a heron. All very Norfolk. And in one of the bedrooms, a Hugh Brandon-Cox painting of Brent geese in a Norfolk sky. "They fascinate me", he confessed. "I just have to keep painting them".

Tens of thousands of swirling, cackling Brent geese arrive in North Norfolk each autumn, escaping the harsh weather of their Russian arctic breeding grounds. They are described by the NWT as 'confiding' and 'conversational', which suggests they are both fascinating and appealing. On the Russian tundra, they are hunted by arctic foxes, though the lemmings are often more plentiful, and cannot fly away. In Norfolk, they are safe, and a cause of delight to thousands of birders, as they were to the late Hugh Brandon-Cox.

I have stated that there are so many excellent wildlife reserves in Norfolk. In addition to the flagship reserve at Cley, others of real note include Strumpshaw fen, where Wendy and I have seen bitterns a few times, Pensthorpe (often used by Springwatch), Titchwell marsh (coastal birds, plus I found chickpea curry on their café menu. Delicious), Blakeney marshes, and Hickling broad and marshes.

*******

Wonderful Norfolk, magnificent throughout the seasons in scenery, wildlife, and activities, has given this Norfolk bor, joy, excitement, wonder, awe, delight, and a wealth of treasured memories covering my nearly 8 decades, at the time of writing. So, under Norfolk's big blue sky, let the adventure continue.

# Thank You

I have mentioned in the Introduction, that I am a 'Norfolk Bor', and that in this county, bors come in all ages, and sometimes, in both sexes. My mother would have been totally bemused, if not offended, if someone had addressed her with the greeting, 'Yew awlroight, bor?'. But the mothers of some of my childhood friends would not have thought twice about it. They might even have responded with, 'Yeah, Oi'm awlroight. Yew awlroight bor?'. And that to the woman who had just delivered the first greeting to her!

I was once a young bor, and maybe three decades later, a middle-aged bor. Today, some would call me an old bor, and I would hope, sometimes, a good ole bor. So I've been around a while, which means that a large number of people, or bors, have passed through my life. These bors have enriched me, and I trust that they have enriched you too, as they have strolled across the pages of this book. I am indebted to them; those from my early years, such as Maud and Gassie, my childhood friends with weird names - Shadley, Sludge, and Gully, to name but a few - and others encountered on my journey of life, going by names such as Mucker and Tater.

They were part of my life for a while, and I thank them. But even more so, my parents, known to so many as Dick and Brenda, who were pillars of stability, and who gave me a secure home, family environment, and childhood. Likewise, my sister Julia. With the perspective of time, I realise how badly and mercilessly I teased her during our childhood. And yet today, decades later, and still not seeing quite eye to eye on some matters, we phone each other frequently and visit often. Julia has been an integral, positive part of my life for nearly eight decades, and I thank her for her patience - and love.

And then one or two local characters I can name and say Thank-you to, for giving me interesting information during conversations, probably without even realising it. Philip Norton, Roger Goodson, Richard Fisher, Ian Douglas, Stephen Hagon, and Worzel immediately come to mind. Norfolk countrymen, engaging conversationists, mines of information, and the salt of the earth.

I enjoy writing, which is a hobby more than a business. Yet, without the help of others more gifted than me, the text would not flow with such clarity and fluency. I refer to my wife Wendy, who proofread the manuscript more than a few times, and my old school friend Barry Harvey, who scrutinises the script, and supplies me with pages of corrections and suggestions. I am indebted. A huge thank you to both.

Grandchild Jasper stepped forward with enthusiasm, to volunteer sketches, with which to add another dimension to the book. Great - we are keeping it in the family. Thank you so much, Jasper.

Derek Blois has designed the cover of every one of my books, although the *Farsi* edition of *A DENTISTS STORY* was produced and published in Iran. The cover design? They really should have asked Derek, who has become an esteemed celebrity artist, both within the county, and much further afield. Once again, I am so very grateful to him, for his time, skill, and friendship.

Biddles, the printers in Kings Lynn, are so easy and helpful to work with, and without the involvement of Bittern Books, Norfolk book distributor and wholesaler, my tomes would not find their way into so many of the literary emporia that display and retail them.

A great big Thank-you to Wendy! Those who know her at all well, have given her the name *Wonder Woman Wendy*, and abbreviate her to www. Which is an understatement, of course, as she never ceases to amaze. Our work with the church and various Christian projects, fellowships, gatherings, etc. sees us hosting, and her feeding, quite large numbers of people at our home here in rural Norfolk. And in addition to all that, and looking after me, she patiently sits besides me as I tap, tap tap away on my tablet, and then vanish to tidy up on the synchronised copy on the desktop in my study. As mentioned above, she proofreads and brings corrections and suggestions; she encourages further writing, and accompanies me to our wholesaler, and to innumerable meetings at which I have spoken about Norfolk, and on many other subjects. Without Wendy, there would probably have been no books. There are no words with which to adequately and properly thank her. And I love her with all my heart.

I make no secret of the fact that I am a practising Christian. My life was so radically changed back in October 1965, and since then, my biggest daily Thankyou has been to Jesus, whose love permeates all of my life. And so I acknowledge and thank the God who gives me creativity and joy as I write.

And finally, there is you, the reader. To each one, I would say, "Thank you, bor, for reading this little treasury of Norfolk", and I know that so many of you have read other books with my name on the cover. Bless you, and maybe you would like to mention them to your friends!

If you've enjoyed ***TALES FROM A COUNTRY BOY***

be sure and read the Companion Volume –

## BIG BLUE SKY – A Celebration of Norfolk

by Barrie Lawrence

Published 2022

RURAL NORFOLK in the postwar years is the setting for childhood adventures with Sludge, Shadley, and Roger the Rough. Catching mice barehanded under haystacks, a pet frog in the bedroom, and trudging over water meadows to trap coypu, gave way to later romantic episodes with Sarah and Cindy on a local fruit farm. Had school discipline really changed since Nelson had been a pupil? Was the sky really so blue? And then to the big city for a spell, where the Norfolk accent was more than a curiosity.

After a 70 year romance with the county, Barrie reflects upon the rural charm of characters, accent, the history, and country life. You'll laugh, you'll cry, and when you've finished reading, you will want more.

*Available from www.amazon.co.uk in the United Kingdom, Waterstones, Jarrolds (Norwich), and all good bookshops.*

***

Barrie Lawrence distils his 70-year love affair with Norfolk. A Norfolk read for a rainy day.

***Norfolk Magazine***. *Review by Rowan Mantell.*

'An unstoppable author, Barrie turns his attention to the mostly amusing sides of life in his beloved Norfolk.'

***Network Norwich***. *Review by Keith Morris.*

# OTHER BOOKS BY BARRIE LAWRENCE

## ANECDOTAL, LIGHT, HUMOROUS

*******

## CURIOUS PEOPLE, HUMOROUS HAPPENINGS, CROWNS OF GLORY

# A DENTIST'S STORY

stories by Barrie Lawrence

Published by Grosvenor House Publishing (2014)

After-dinner speaker Barrie Lawrence has been making people laugh - *really* laugh - for years. Now it's your turn to hear his unbelievably funny, sometimes poignant stories from dental school, surgery and life. How did a pet frog lead to a successful career of seven dental surgeries and a bookshop? And of course, he was a student during those years known as the 'Swinging Sixties!'

*"A refreshing delight. The author succeeds in maintaining interest by careful selection of anecdotes combined with a light-hearted tone and appropriate pace. I would recommend this book to anybody... looking for something uncomplicated and entertaining".*

**British Dental Journal**, *Review by T. Doshi, December 2014*

# PATIENTS FROM HEAVEN – and Other Places!

## By Barrie Lawrence

## Published by Grosvenor House (2015)

Baron Goldfinger seemed to have stepped straight off the James Bond movie set, Tad the Pole caused the nurses to swoon, while Misty, the flirtatious American lady, suddenly vanished – probably murdered, said the police. These and dozens of other colourful characters walk across the pages of *Patients From Heaven – and Other Places!* During nearly forty years of practice in dental surgery, a wealth of fascinating personalities passed through his surgery. Some were from heaven - and some were from other places! Laugh, smile, gasp, cry, and simply be inspired as you read through these engaging from real life.

*"Barrie introduces us to some of the most memorable people he met in this lovely and engaging memoir, the follow-up of his well-received A Dentist's Story. This is a lively read – he has a real way with a tale that keeps you turning the pages. Barrie is a practising Christian, but he doesn't hit you over the head with it; only mentioning it 'as and when' to put his story into context. An enjoyable – and rather uplifting – read".*

**Eastern Daily Press**, *Review by Trevor Heaton, June 2015*

# LICENSED TO DRILL – Dentist on the Loose!

## By Barrie Lawrence

## Published by Grosvenor House (2015)

Licensed to drill! Shots, Killing, Out Cold, Asphyxiated, Agents, Accomplices, Cocaine, the Opposition, The Man with the Golden Tooth, Heroes, Villains and a trip to Russia in the days of the old Soviet Union all figure in this fascinating catalogue of stories from nearly 40 years of being LICENSED TO DRILL!

See just what really goes on at times behind the doors of a dental practice. Three patients fled, one with the dentist in hot pursuit. Fruit pastilles were laced with anaesthetic, and on one occasion, a 'dangerous mongoose' escaped from its cage in the car park. And so much more.

Barrie takes the lid off life in a dental practice in a way that is engaging, entertaining, and totally unforgettable.

*Former Norfolk dentist Dr. Lawrence delves into 40 years of stories to come up with his third collection of anecdotes. When it comes to the dentist's chair, all human life is there, and Barrie has met many, many kinds of people over the years; the man who insisted on having a gold filling as an investment (it wasn't) to one who was convinced – like that famous Tommy Cooper gag come to life – that his 'teeth itched' (they didn't). As with all of Barrie's books, this is lively, chatty stuff and a very easy (and rather informative) read.*

**Eastern Daily Press**. *Review by Trevor Heaton, May 2017*

# Also by Barrie Lawrence – Christian Faith

## THERE MUST BE MORE TO LIFE THAN THIS!
### How to know the God of the Bible in Everyday Life

by Barrie Lawrence

Published by New Wine Press (2012)

Barrie writes in his own distinctive style of incidents in his life that can only be described as amazing coincidences – or acts of God!

*A brilliant book by Barrie Lawrence. For anyone asking, **'Is there more to life than this?'** the author reveals a resounding 'Yes'. He shares his own journey of faith with refreshing candour – and then shows how the reader can experience Life with a capital L.*

**Michael Wiltshire**, *author and journalist, and a director of FGB, the world's largest fellowship for Christian businessmen.*

# THE CURIOUS CASE OF THE CONSTIPATED CAT
## – and Other True Stories of Answered Prayer

by Barrie Lawrence

Published by Grosvenor House (2016)

A terminally constipated pussy cat, two frozen shoulders, a man with a broken arm, a boy with a deformed arm, broken relationships, work overload, lost at night in a foreign city, irritable bowel, Crohn's Disease, financial challenges, wanting a husband, wanting a wife, not wanting divorce... All these needs were met after prayer. Coincidences? Psychosomatic? Don't be so silly. Come on - get real! Barrie and Wendy Lawrence, two very ordinary people, say, "If He can do it for us, then He can do it for you".

*"It's not the most conventional title for a Christian book. But then Barrie Lawrence is no average author. The Curious Case of the Constipated Cat and Other True Stories of Answered Prayer is the fourth book penned by Mr. Lawrence, a dentist, author and speaker. The book is different because not many 'religious books' are written in (his) style. Well, look at the title for a start! It is a collection of true stories of answered prayer, ranging from a cat being cured of constipation, and fog suddenly lifting so a flight could take off, to a troubled marriage being saved".*

**Eastern Daily Press**. *Review by Ian Clarke, 26th March 2016*

*"Feel your faith rise as you read these stories of answered prayer - faith to reach out to the God who can meet your need too."*

**Don Double, Evangelist and Founder, Good News Crusade.**

# PENNIES FROM HEAVEN
## How To Get Them and What To Do With Them

by Barrie Lawrence

Published by Grosvenor House (2018)

**Money, Dosh, Dough**. We all need it, but – how do we get it? This book tells you HOW! And having got it, what do we do with it?

Is it difficult to make ends meet? Are you on the edge of a financial abyss? Perhaps you really need a financial miracle. Barrie has been in all those places and more, and with Jesus as his supply, has come through.

The Bible has a lot to say about money, and Barrie has also learnt much from failure and success. Using Biblical principles and a wealth of personal illustrations, he shows you HOW you too, whilst avoiding the prosperity cult, can enjoy Biblical prosperity.

*Readers will need to be prepared for Barrie's challenges with heartbreak, wealth, financial devastation, time, relationships and "I would never have dreamed of the wonderful surprises that lay in store for me."*

*Review from Network Norwich by Kevin Gotts.*